MADRAS

THE BIRTH PLACE OF BRITISH INDIA

H. A. NEWELL

GYAN

Published by

Gyan Publishing House
5, Ansari Road
Daryaganj, New Delhi-110002
Phone: 011-47034999, 9811692060
E-mail: books@gyanbooks.com

Distribution Network
gyanbooks.com
India, USA, Canada, UK, Australia

ISBN: 978-93-6780-373-8 (HB)

First Published, 1919

2nd Impression 2024

Printed at: Gyan Press, Delhi.

MADRAS THE BIRTH PLACE OF BRITISH INDIA
Author: H. A. NEWELL

MADRAS

THE BIRTH PLACE OF BRITISH INDIA

MADRAS

THE BIRTH PLACE OF BRITISH INDIA

AN ILLUSTRATED GUIDE WITH MAP

BY

LIEUT.-COLONEL H. A. NEWELL, F.R.G.S.,
INDIAN ARMY.

MADRAS:
PRINTED AT THE MADRAS TIMES PRINTING & PUBLG. CO., LD.
1919.

CONTENTS

ILLUSTRATIONS

INTRODUCTION.

Claim is made that British connection with Madras dates as far back as the ninth century A. D. According to the Anglo-Saxon Chronicle, and to the further testimony of William of Malmesbury, King Alfred the Great of England despatched two ambassadors, Sighelm and Athelstane, in 883, with alms to Rome, and thence to St. Thomas in India. The identification of the latter place has never presented any difficulty. From early Christian times the old quarter of Madras, known as Mylapore, has been associated with the name of the "Doubting Apostle." That St. Thomas visited the Court of the Indo-Scythian sovereign Gondophares, in the far North-West, is now generally admitted. The fact that a colony of Christians, styling themselves his followers, existed in South India in the fourth century may be held to confirm the belief that he also lived and laboured in that part of the Coromandel Coast, where his memory has so long been piously preserved.

At the beginning of the Christian era Mylapore is reputed to have been a large and prosperous city, the capital of a Hindu Raja. Tradition likewise asserts that the sea has since encroached some three miles or so, swallowing up the ancient metropolis, a disaster foretold by St. Thomas, who took the precaution to build his small Church well inland, on the site now covered by the large Cathedral, which bears his name. A miracle, whereby the Apostle restored the Raja's daughter to health, when she lay at the point of death, so incensed the local Brahmins, that he fled to a cave on the Little Mount, near the mouth of the Adyar River. His retreat was speedily discovered. He was attacked and wounded. Seeking refuge once more in flight he dragged himself as far as the Great Mount. There he was finally despatched by a spear thrust on December 21st, A. D. 68.

Early in the sixteenth century the pious associations of the place attracted a number of Portuguese settlers to Mylapore. After founding Churches, monasteries and convents on sites hallowed by association with the Apostle, they proceeded to erect and fortify the city of San Thomé.

Material rather than spiritual considerations brought the English to Madras a century later. For them the neighbourhood possessed the coveted distinction of producing cheap and excellent muslins and printed calicoes. This induced Francis Day, the East India Company's Agent at Armegam, the fortified English factory established in 1628 near Masulipatam in the territory of Golcondah, to urge its abandonment in favour of a more advantageous site further south, offered, in 1639, by the Naik of Chingleput. The latter wished to attract trade to his own district, hence the easy terms upon which he proposed to lease the small seaport town of Madraspatam to the merchants.

Acting largely on their own responsibility Andrew Cogan, the Company's Agent at Masulipatam, and Francis Day proceeded to build a factory at Madraspatam and enclose it with a battlemented wall. They dignified the new establishment with the name of Fort St. George, England's patron saint, inspired, probably, by the close proximity of the rival Portuguese settlement of San Thomé, three miles to the south.

The small English community in Madras struggled on with, apparently, little encouragement from anyone. Blame rather than praise seems to have been their portion at home while, abroad, they were surrounded by enemies. Possibly this explains the hardihood of their growth. Immediately to south their boundary trespassed upon the Portuguese territory of San Thomé. The dreaded Dutch threatened them from Pulicat, Negapatam, Masulipatam and Sadras. The last mentioned places were founded about 1610 and held by Holland until 1824, when they were finally ceded to England. In 1620 the Danes started to trade at Tranquebar. They attained little commercial, or political importance. Their chief achievement consisted in establishing the earliest Protestant missions in India. It was they who welcomed William Carey, the first Baptist missionary from England, and allowed him to settle at Serampur in 1799, under the protection of their Governor, Colonel Bie. Prior to this the English East India Company had refused to allow Carey to proselytize within their territories. Finally, the French began to erect and fortify Pondicherry, an advantageously situated seaport, lower down on the Coromandel Coast. Founded by Francis Martin, in April 1674, it speedily grew into the handsomest European town in India.

Cities, like men, are the product of their past. How the merchant venturers at Fort St. George held their own against enemies at home and abroad, how they beat back the Moghuls, and the Marathas, and how, while merely seeking to extend their trade, they were, all unwittingly, building up an empire upon such apparently incongruous foundations as bales of cotton, and bags of spice, is the story of Madras. In the following pages I have endeavoured to outline the tale. In the very limited space of a little guide book I do not pretend to exhaust the subject but merely to arouse interest therein.

For information regarding the harbour I am indebted to the kindness of Sir Francis Spring.

H. A. NEWELL,
LIEUT.-COLONEL,
Indian Army.

MADRAS,
April, 1919.

MADRAS.

Into the comparatively short period of three hundred years Madras has crowded an important and varied history, marked by events which have exercised a far-reaching influence upon the British-Indian Empire in particular, and the world in general. Madras was a power in the land before Bombay was transferred to England as a Queen's dower, Calcutta founded, or Karachi thought of. With the exception of an insignificant piece of ground at Armegam, in the Kistna district, it was the earliest territory acquired by the Honourable East India Company, and, for some time, the only stronghold worthy the name which they possessed. By virtue of these facts, Madras is senior of the three great Presidencies, and her Governor ranks second only to the Viceroy.

At the beginning of the seventeenth century the present large and scattered city, comprising a municipal area of some twenty-seven miles, and a seafront nine miles in extent, consisted of a number of big villages, small kuppams, or fishing hamlets, and the ancient Hindu town of Mylapore, which included the Portuguese settlement of San Thomé. As Madras expanded all these old sites were gradually absorbed. Their names, however, persisted and still designate the various districts into which they have developed, hence such appellations as Nungumbakum, Tondiarpet, Peddanaickenpet, etc., formidable mouthfuls to strangers unfamiliar with Tamil and allied Dravidian languages. Nor are these the sole survivals from the dim past. Despite the roadmaker and the builder, primeval palm topes persist in unexpected places. Aboriginal kuppams make picturesque appeal on the bare sandy foreshore or hidden amid the green of trees. Their mud walls, and the design of their sloping thatched roofs are the same today as they were before the calendar was invented. The centuries have wrought no change in the catamarans constructed, raft-like, by lashing together the roughly hewn trunks of trees. In these crude craft the fisher folk continue to breast the surf with a skill tantamount to instinct, and which is a legacy from remote antiquity. Antediluvian, too, are the large hollow masoolah-boats, built up of thin planks stitched in place with a tough kind of fibrous rope. They lie on the beach below, while above, on the smooth Marina, beyond the yellow blossomed portia trees, modern civilisation speeds swiftly along in motor cars, under the watchful windows of imposing Government buildings, and of new and up-to-date educational establishments. It is to contrasts such as these that Madras owes much of its charm.

The first European settlement in the neighbourhood dates from early in the sixteenth century, and was Portuguese. Its origin was religious. In 1498 the Portuguese navigator, Vasco de Gama, revolutionised existing geographical theories by doubling the Cape of Good Hope, and so discovering a sea route to India. He penetrated as far as Calicut, on the West Coast, and obtained a charter from the Zamorin permitting his countrymen to trade. In 1502 a papal bull proclaimed the King of Portugal "Lord of the navigation, conquests and trade of Ethiopia, Arabia, Persia and India." As a result, a Portuguese crown colony was established at Goa, the first Viceroy of which was Francisco di Almeda. Reports reaching Goa that St. Thomas the "Doubting Apostle," had suffered martyrdom on a mount near Mylapore, on the Coromandel Coast, officials were despatched to verify the tradition. Royal sanction was obtained from Portugal for the establishment of churches and monasteries on sites hallowed by association with the Apostle. According to the "Madras Manual," Francis di Albuquerque had already founded a factory at San Thomé in 1603. Soon a Portuguese city sprang up around a shrine, which the Saint is said to have built on the ground now covered by the Cathedral named after him. Fortifications perforce followed. A garrison and commandant were despatched from Goa, by the Viceroy, to whom the new settlement was subject.

Of the indigenous villages the two earliest to come within the sphere of English influence appear to have been Chinnapatam, or Chennapatnam (Fair Town) and Madraspatam. These lay on the foreshore about three miles north of San Thomé. Various theories have been advanced regarding the origin of the two names. The former is generally believed to have been so styled in honour of Chenappa, father of the Naik of Chingleput, who invited the English to build a factory in the neighbourhood. Scholars consider that Madraspatam perpetuates the memory of a legendary king of the Solar Line. The locality produced cheap and excellent cotton fabrics, notably stamped calicoes. Many of the inhabitants were skilled weavers.

This speciality attracted the attention of traders, and induced Francis Day, an Agent of the East India Company incorporated by Queen Elizabeth on December 31st, 1600, to remove the English factory from Armegam to a place affording more favourable opportunities for commercial development.

THE NAIK'S OFFER.

At this epoch the district was subject to a descendant of the once great Hindu dynasty of Vijianagar, the paramount power in South India during the fourteenth and fifteenth centuries. Founded A. D. 1336 the Vijianagar empire was shattered in 1564 by the combined armies of the Muhammadan Kings of the Deccan. The battle of Talikottah proved final. Ram Raja was slain and his splendid capital wrecked. His successors established their head-quarters at Chandragiri, seventy miles north-west of Madras, in the present collectorate of North Arcot. Here they continued for some time. Under them Telugu was the State language. Their claim to Hindu supremacy was acknowledged, although not always respected, by the various local Naiks, or Governors.

With the consent of the Raja, the Naik of Chingleput, a man of progressive views who desired to attract trade to his province, entered into negotiations with Francis Day regarding the establishment of a fortified English factory "in, or about Madraspatam." The Company's Agents reported the proceedings in a letter dated from Masulipatam on October 25th, 1639. They wrote :—"The Naik of that place is very desirous of our residence there, for he hath made us very fair proffers to that effect. First he proffers to build a fort, in what manner we please, upon a high plot of ground adjoining the sea, where a ship of any burthen may ride within musket shot close by a river capable of a vessel of fifty tons, and upon possession given us by him, and not before, to pay what charges he shall have disbursed. Secondly, he gives us the whole benefit of a town near by for two years, which town may be at present worth about two thousand pagodas per annum, but after two years the proceeds of that town to be equally divided between him and us. Thirdly, we to be custom free continually at the port of Madras, and if we carry our goods through his country to pay half the custom usually paid by other merchants. Fourthly, we to enjoy the privilege of minting without paying any dues. Fifthly, that for all such money as we shall deliver out to workmen he, the said Naik, will be liable to make it good provided he be acquainted with the delivery. Sixthly, that whatsoever provisions we shall buy, either for Fort or shipping, to pay no duties at all. Lastly, if any ship, or vessel (belonging to us or our friends) be cast upon any of his territories, all goods saved will, upon demand, be delivered to us.

They are fair privileges, and it may be questioned why he should make us these fair proffers. 'Tis answered by himself. First, he desires his country may grow rich, which he conceives it will by drawing merchants to him. Secondly, he desires good horses from Persia. Thirdly, that, yearly, upon our ships he may send a servant into the Bay Bengalla to buy him hawks, apes, parrots and such like baubles; and that, when he shall have occasion to send a vessel of his own there, or to Persia, a man of ours may proceed upon her. And, lastly, the fort being made strong and substantial, may be able to defend his person on occasion against his insulting neighbours."

Day's description of the natural advantages of Madraspatam was somewhat rose-coloured. The high plot of land, which he recommended as a desirable site, and the one upon which Fort St. George was subsequently built, consisted of a surf bank raised a few feet only above the low lying tract to westward. As to the sea "where a ship of any burthen may ride at anchor within musket shot," it was an open roadstead exposed to dangerous winds and a strong current. The continuous rough surf, breaking upon the sandy beach, rendered landing, or putting out a matter of extreme difficulty and no small peril. As for the river close by, "capable of a vessel of fifty tons," it was navigable by none but a flat bottomed boat of this tonnage. The fifth clause refers to the advances, which the Company's Agents made to weavers, on account of goods that were not always delivered.

Venkatappa, the Naik of Chingleput, controlled the Coromandel coast from Pulicat to San Thomé. The merchants describe him as Lord of the Carnatic and Commander of from twelve to fifteen thousand troops. He appears to have chiefly resided at Chandragiri, or else at Wandiwash, about sixty miles from Madras, famous, later on, as the scene of Coote's victory over Lally. His brother, Ayappa Naik, lived at Poonamallee, at which place he is said to have discussed conditions with Day. Eventually a gold-plated kaul was executed empowering the English to erect a fort, and castle, "in or about Madraspatam." When sanctioning the grant, the Raja of Vijianagar stipulated that the new settlement should be styled Srirangapatnam after himself. No attention seems to have been paid to this clause.

Up to date the English had not secured any important footing in South India. Their chief bases were at Surat, in Gujarat, on the West Coast and at Bantam. At the former port they were seriously hampered by the exactions of the Moghul Governor, and the rivalry of Portuguese competitors. In Java they were fiercely opposed by the Dutch, who were determined to preserve Holland's monopoly of the spice trade.

The Honourable East India Company despatched their seventh expedition to the Orient in 1610. Their ship *Globe*, commanded by Captain Hippon, sailed up the East Coast, reaching Pettapolly, now Nizampatam in the Kistna district, on August 20th, 1611. Goods were landed in charge of two supercargoes. The *Globe* then proceeded to Masulipatam. In 1621 factories were established at both these ports. Seven years later a third was erected at Armegam and fortified by a weak wall and twelve guns. Francis Day was appointed Agent subject to Masulipatam and Bantam.

During the next few years rival European associations multiplied their depôts in Asia. The result was that trade competition between representatives of the various western nations led to friction, and even to armed conflicts.

Francis Day was thoroughly dissatisfied with conditions at Armegam. No sooner did he receive the Naik of Chingleput's offer than he started for Masulipatam to confer with Thomas Ivie, Agent at that port and Superintendent of the Coast factories. Upon arrival he learnt that Ivie had been superseded by Andrew Cogan, one time a member of Council at Surat. Letters were despatched to Bantam requesting permission to close with the Naik's offer. Writing from Armegam, in 1639, Day urged:—" I acquainted you with many kind invitations and large privileges by the Naik of Vincaladre, whose territories lie between Pulicat and San Thomé, the only place for paintings so much admired at southward (*i.e.*, at Bantam) and likewise store of longcloth and morrees which is there procurable."

Day's proposals were favourably regarded by the agents and factors assembled at Masulipatam. On September 5th, 1630, Thomas Ivie, Andrew Cogan, Francis Day, Thomas Winter and Thomas Morris met to discuss the question. In the record of the proceedings Madraspatam is described as a "port town between Pulicat and San Thomé."* Mention is again made of the cloth and "paintings," otherwise stamped cottons, for which the neighbourhood was celebrated, and which rendered it preeminently desirable in the merchant's eyes. Pending an answer, news was received that the coast factories were no longer under Bantam, but were to take their orders from Surat. Eventually a letter came from that place, dated January 8th, 1640. In this the Council appear to have taken it for granted that the East Coast factors had acted upon their own initiative as they remark "Fortifying at Madraspatam will be so far advanced that our directions will come too late to improve the action."

ARMEGAM ABANDONED.

On February 6th, 1640, this somewhat ambiguously worded document reached Armegam. Immediately the work of dismantlement commenced. Shortly afterwards Cogan, Day and the *personnel* of the abandoned fort embarked in three ships, two of which, the *Unity* and *Eagle*, are respectively described as of one hundred tons burthen. The little company included two or three factors, an equal number of writers, a gunner, a surgeon, several carpenters, smiths and coopers, an Indian powder maker, a staff of servants, and the European garrison, about twenty-five strong, commanded by a Lieutenant, assisted by a Sergeant. All reached their destination safely on February 20th.

When approached regarding his offer to erect a fort, the Naik of Chingleput responded that his intention was limited to throwing up a stockade of toddy palms and earth. At this the merchants decided to do their own building. The work began on March 1st, 1840, but was greatly hampered by lack of funds, and so dragged on for nearly fourteen years. The site chosen was a surf bank between the sea, on the east, and the Elambore River, now known as the Cooum, on the west. Day and Cogan commenced by erecting a square three-storeyed edifice containing warehouses, offices and quarters for the staff. This was surrounded by a courtyard and four battlemented walls, with bastions at the corners and as many batteries.

EARLY DAYS.

At first the Company's employees had no better dwelling than palm huts on the beach. Disaster speedily overtook the new settlement. Within three weeks of its foundation a cyclone wrecked the *Unity* and drove the *Eagle* ashore. Unseasonable rains followed, greatly retarding building operations. In order to attract a population the merchants promised thirty years immunity from taxation "upon anything to eat, to drink, or to wear." By the end of 1640 nearly four hundred families of weavers had established themselves in the vicinity, likewise a number of Portuguese from San Thomé. Before long houses sprang up around the Castle, or Factory as Fort St. George was variously designated. These in turn, were gradually hemmed in by ramparts forming an outer fort, the inner enclosure being converted into a citadel. The outer enceinte was almost entirely inhabited by Europeans, hence the name of Christian, or White Town so frequently applied to it. Beyond the curtain to north stretched a wide thoroughfare termed General Market. This constituted the southern boundary of Gentu, or Black Town, in its turn, safeguarded by walls of mud.

NOMENCLATURE.

The fact that Madras is still locally styled Chinnapatam has led Colonel Love, R. E., to form certain conclusions, which are both interesting and valuable as he bases them upon official records. In his opinion a place named Madraspatam existed prior to the advent of Day and Cogan. He further believes that the new town, which grew up around Fort St. George, was called Chinnapatam by inhabitants of the country, and was regarded as distinct from Madraspatam by Vijianagar, in 1645, and Golcondah, in 1672. He considers that the site of Fort St. George lay within the limits of Chinnapatam, to south of Madraspatam. In support of this he cites Doctor Fryer's Map, drawn in 1673, wherein "Madirass, the Indian town with flat houses" is shown immediately to north. Although originally separate, Colonel Love holds that the intervening space between Chinnapatam and Madraspatam was gradually built over uniting the two villages and converting them into one city, to which the English gave the name of Madras, while the Indians preferred that of Chinnapatam. The old quarter, designated Black Town, has been cleared away. Part of it is now occupied by the tall posts of the wireless station. The densely populated area known as George Town was so styled in honour of the King-Emperor's visit as Prince of Wales in 1906.

FOUNDERS OF FORT ST. GEORGE.

Very soon Day was recalled to England to answer charges of having advanced his own interests by private trading, to the prejudice of those of the Company. During his absence Cogan promoted Fort St. George to be chief of the coast factories in lieu of Masulipatam, which was held under a far less favourable grant from the Sultan of Golcondah. In their annual report, dated September 1642, Cogan, H. Greenhill and J. Brown complain of their neighbours at San Thomé. They describe the Portuguese Garrison as turbulent and undisciplined, and accuse three Portuguese soldiers of having come over into the Company's territory, where, after drinking with a Dane in a local arrack shop, they fell upon the unfortunate man and killed him. For this the factors seized the principal offender and shot him in front of the main guard to west of the Fort House. Shortly afterwards the *Hopewell* arrived from England bearing despatches from the Company. Cogan was sharply reprimanded for the loss of the *Eagle* and for founding Fort St. George. Meanwhile the surrounding country was in a distracted condition owing to disputes between the governors of provinces and their sovereign, the Raja of Vijianagar. Matters were complicated by the Muhammadans, who took advantage of the situation to advance upon Hindu territory. Among the rebels was the Governor of Chingleput, or "Our Great Naique," as the factors styled him. The Raja caused him to be seized and imprisoned, much to the consternation of the English merchants, who promptly applied for more, and heavier guns, wherewith to protect their own persons, and the Company's possessions.

In the midst of these alarms Cogan handed over the Agency to Day, in 1643. The latter had been reinstated. Cogan then sailed for Bantam *en route* for England, where, upon arrival, he was summoned before the Court of Directors, charged wlth building a factory at Madraspatam. In his defence he stated the work had made such good progress before he left that the house or tower in the middle was finished, likewise three of the corner bulwarks, adding that thirty-four pieces of ordnance had been mounted. He was acquitted, and Francis Day pronounced responsible should the venture not prove a success. With this Cogan retired after twenty-eight years service. He settled at Greenwich, where he purchased Crowley House, and was knighted. In politics he was a stout supporter of the Royalist cause,. After the Restoration, Charles II conferred a baronetcy on him in 1657.

Hardly had Day been appointed Agent at Fort St. George than he applied to be relieved. His successor, Thomas Ivie, took over from him, on August 4th, 1644, Day promptly sailed for England, where the Company fined him £500 for private trading. Nothing is known of his subsequent history, a curious fate to befall the founder of so great and important a city as Madras.

TRANSFER TO GOLCONDAH.

Thomas Ivie directed the affairs of the Agency during four critical years. The failure of the north-east monsoon caused a famine of such severity that in Madras alone four thousand died of hunger. The Raja of Vijianagar was mulcted of the major portion of his remaining possessions by the Sultan of Golcondah, whose great Prime Minister, Mir Jumlah, proceeded to blockade San Thomé in 1646. Anxious to propitiate the rising power, and also, possibly, to pay off old scores against their Portuguese neighbours, the English assisted in the attack for a brief period.

Henry Greenhill was the next Agent. Like his predecessors he sought to promote good relations with Mir Jumlah who, in 1647, had used his influence to have the merchants confirmed in their tenure of Madras. The conditions of the lease were not finally settled until 1672 when it was agreed that the traders should pay eleven thousand pagodas down in settlement of arrears, and an annual tribute to the Sultan of Golcondah of one thousand two hundred pagodas, otherwise Rs. 4,800. Beyond this they were to be exempt from further imposition whatsoever for all time.

Mir Jumlah responded to Greenhill's advances by desiring to become a shareholder in the Company, and so participate in the profits. To this end he offered to invest sixty thousand pagodas. The factors describe the extensive trade carried on by Mir Jumlah on his own account. They enumerate his ten merchant ships, his four thousand horses, three hundred camels and ten thousand oxen, all engaged in transporting his wares to different towns, in each of which he had agencies.

MADRAS A PRESIDENCY.

In 1652 Fort St. George was declared the Company's eastern centre of Government. Consequently President Aaron Baker was ordered from Java to Madras, where he arrived on September 1st. His wife died during the voyage. A tombstone to her memory forms part of the pavement to the north-east of the narrow enclosure surrounding St. Mary's Church, and is the oldest British monument of the kind in the city. Upon Baker superseding him, Greenhill vacated his quarters in the Inner Fort, and went to live in a house that he had built in White Town. He continued to act as Agent, with the result that disputes between him and President Baker were frequent and embittered. War breaking out with Holland, efforts were made to strengthen the defences of Fort St. George. Dutch records of the period describe how the English erected a kind of bastion, towards the sea, flanked by a dozen cannon.

Early in 1655 Aaron Baker retired to England, purchased a property at Exminster, and built a mansion that was unfortunately destroyed by fire in 1838. Greenhill succeeded him, but it was a troubled heritage. The Court of Directors decided to close the small factories and reduce the large ones. Fort St. George was again declared an Agency subject to Surat. Meanwhile Mir Jumlah had deserted the cause of his old sovereign, the Sultan of Golcondah, and espoused that of the Moghul Prince, Aurangzib. His withdrawal from the Carnatic led to a Hindu revolt, during which the Raja of Vijianagar sought to re-establish his power. Exasperated by the exactions of Bala Rao, Governor of Poonamallee, the English joined in the fray by seizing a junk belonging to Mir Jumlah, which lay off San Thomé. The prize proved of little value, whereas the results for the factors were disastrous in the extreme. Not only were they called upon to defend themselves against two attacks in the immediate neighbourhood, but Mir Jumlah sought to take vengeance upon them in Bengal. In the midst of these troubles Greenhill died of dropsy in 1659. He was buried in the graveyard at Black Town, on the site now occupied by the Law College. An engraved tablet to his memory, believed to have been removed from there to the Fort, is let into the outer wall of St. Mary's Church, near the north-east angle below the spire.

Sir Thomas Chamber was the next Agent. He quarrelled with the authorities at Surat, was suspended and dismissed the Company's service, whereupon he retired to England, was knighted and purchased an estate at Bromley, in Kent.

After him came Sir Edward Winter, whose appointment was a personal triumph. He had been recalled to England to answer various charges, that of private trading among the number. So well did he present his case that Charles II conferred a title upon him, and the Court of Directors sent him back to Madras as Agent. He arrived in the autumn of 1662. Possessed of much independence of character he promptly set about enlarging the Castle, strengthening the Fort, and reinforcing the garrison.

Peace was concluded with Holland in 1663. Mir Jumlah had died in the previous year, but, as his connection with Golcondah had long been severed, this event did not affect Madras. Meanwhile the Muhammadans maintained a strong garrison at San Thomé, "so that we are in danger of our lives if we do but go out further than the reach of our guns," wrote Sir Edward Winter in 1663.

THE FIRST GOVERNOR.

Fresh charges being brought against Winter, the Court of Directors sent out Mr. George Foxcroft to relieve him. The new Agent was accompanied by his son, Nathaniel, and arrived at Madras in June, 1663. He at once assumed office, with Sir Edward Winter as Second in Council. Soon Foxcroft discovered that his predecessor's accounts showed him to be in debt to the Company. Furthermore, he found that the alleged wages paid to weavers were greatly in excess of what they actually received. Awkward questions followed. Finding his credit seriously menaced, Winter set about forming a party to support his interests and defy Foxcroft. This was the easier as he was a staunch Royalist, whereas it was public knowledge that, until recently, Foxcroft had been a Cromwellian. In the meantime the murder of a slave girl, and the arrest of her owner, Mrs. Dawes, who was charged with the crime, placed the Agent and the Council in an awkward predicament. Uncertain of their judicial powers they appealed to England for instructions as to how to deal with the case. Before an answer could be received Winter seized Foxcroft. imprisoned him in a small lock-up in the Inner Fort, and usurped control. He justified his mutinous action by charging Foxcroft with having supported his son Nathaniel when the latter uttered alleged treasonable remarks against the King at the public dinner table. The arrest was not effected without bloodshed. Both Foxcroft and his son were wounded, and one man shot dead.

The Agent was still a close prisoner in the following year, when a reply was received, from England, regarding the course to be pursued in respect to the murder of the slave girl. The Company were unaware of the misfortune which had overtaken their Agent, to whom they sent out a fresh commission, sanctioned by Charles II, promoting him to be Governor of Fort St. George, with power to try capital charges. Under such curious and dramatic circumstances was the nomination of the first Governor effected in 1666.

When the Court of Directors eventually learnt of the state of affairs in Madras, a fleet of five ships, and a frigate, were despatched to reinstate Foxcroft and restore order. This was accomplished in August of the same year. No action appears to have been taken against Winter. He remained on in Madras and its neighbourhood winding up his private affairs until 1672. Upon arrival in England he was informed that he would not be allowed to return to India. He installed himself at York House, Battersea, where he died in 1686, and was interred in the Parish

Church, which contains a handsome monument and bust to his memory.

The remainder of Foxcroft's administration was disturbed by disputes with Golcondah over custom dues. The original kaul, executed in 1639, stipulated that the annual customs of Madras should be divided equally between the English and the Raja of Chandragiri, or Vijianagar as he is variously styled. Subsequently Agent Greenhill had prevailed upon Mir Jumlah to agree to a fixed yearly sum of three hundred pagodas. Neknam Khan, on succeeding to office, repudiated this old arrangement. Instead he demanded the whole of the customs, together with the right to place his own official permanently in Madras to check receipts. At that period a brisk traffic was carried on in slaves. A poll tax of one pagoda was levied on all slaves passing through the port with very profitable results.

TRANSFER TO THE MOGHUL EMPIRE.

In 1687 the kingdom of Golcondah was completely subverted by the Moghul Emperor Aurangzib, and the old Sultan treacherously put to death at Daulatabad. Upon this Madras became tributary to the Moghuls. Contrary to expectation, the transfer proved beneficial to the merchants, thanks to a service which they rendered to General Zulfikar Khan, son of Assad Khan, the Delhi Grand Wazir. In 1690 he applied to Fort St. George for two hundred maunds of gunpowder, as he was then subduing the Gingee country. This was sent him and was followed by a further demand, which was also complied with. Zulfikar Khan expressed his gratitude by sending Governor Yale a firman confirming the existing grants for the Fort and Factory of Chinnapatam, together with the Company's other establishments on the Coromandel Coast.

Nevertheless, Yale duly deducted the price of the ammunition from the town rent payable to the Moghul Emperor.

FIRST NAWAB OF THE CARNATIC.

In 1692 Aurangzib created Zulfikar Ali Khan Nawab of the Carnatic, subject to the Subahdar of the Deccan, a post which he continued to hold until 1701, when he was succeeded by Daud Khan. During the first year of his office Zulfikar Khan was joined in his camp at Gingee by his father Assad Khan, the Grand Wazir, and by Prince Kam Baksh, the Emperor's son. On learning of this, Governor Yale despatched Richard Trenchfield and John Pitt to Gingee, with a petition wherein he expatiated upon the powder incident by virtue of which he solicited certain privileges. The chief was that Madras and Triplicane should be held rent free and henceforward exempt from the annual payment of pagodas 1,200. Furthermore, he begged for an extension of territory which should include the villages of Egmore, Pursewaukum and Tondiarpet, the combined annual production of which he assessed at pagodas 300. Finally, he begged leave to coin rupees bearing the Emperor's stamp, at Madras. The last request was granted by Prince Kam Baksh. The other two were submitted to Aurangzib and subsequently sanctioned at a much later date.

JOB CHARNOCK.

The failure of the Company's expedition against Bengal left the Agent, Job Charnock, no option but to withdraw from Hughli and the other northern factories. Accompanied by his entire civil and military staff, he arrived at Fort St. George, on March 7th, 1689. He remained in Madras, as the guest of Governor Yale, for sixteen months, during which time he sat in Council whenever Bengal was in question. Finally, in July 1690, it was decided that he should return and attempt to establish a fresh settlement. A banquet was given in his honour on the 15th. After dinner he and his party embarked in the *Princess* and *Kempthorne*. They then proceeded to Chuttanuttee, where they founded the present city of Calcutta. The Court of Directors acknowledged Charnock's courage and initiative by declaring Bengal independent of Madras during his agency.

RAPID PROGRESS.

As early as 1653 Madras had been raised to the dignity of a Presidency. In 1666 the first Governor was appointed, 1688 witnessed the establishment of a Corporation, consisting of a Mayor, appointed annually on September 29th, twelve Aldermen and sixty or more Burgesses. These were empowered to levy certain taxes in connection with public works, and to try criminal as well as civil causes. The right of appeal against their verdicts was allowed in cases where the offender was fined over three pagodas, or condemned to lose life, or limb. That the dignity of their high office might be apparent to all it was commanded that, on public occasions, two English born sergeants, bearing silver gilt maces, should precede the Mayor, who was to be robed in scarlet serge, accompanied by Aldermen in red gowns, and Burgesses clad in white silk. The Corporation were further entitled to have umbrellas held over them, and to ride on horseback.

Eloquent testimony as to the rapid progress of the settlement comes from the pen of Manucci, the Venetian physician, who arrived at Delhi in 1656 and devoted the next half century to collecting materials for his famous memoirs of the Moghul Court, of the Portuguese at Goa and San Thomé, of the French at Pondicherry and last, but not least, of the English at Madras, where he settled in 1689. Writing in 1699, the celebrated author of the "Storia do Mogor" says :—"Not more than sixty years ago this Madras was a sandy beach in the territory of Golcondah, where the English began by erecting straw huts. In time, by slow degrees, through prudence and good government, they built a fortress, castle and spacious suburbs. By the freedom given to merchants of all nations it is now become very populous. Great profits are earned there. It is very famous and larger than any place on the Coromandel Coast. Merchants throng to it from all parts, it having whatever they are in want of. The ruin of San Thomé was of great benefit to Madras, for its materials were used to extend it."

By the ruin of San Thomé Manucci refers to its dismantlement by the Muhammadans in 1697, when the massive fortifications were blown up and the masonry remains appropriated by the English for building purposes. It was ceded to the Company in 1749 by Muhammad Ali, Nawab of the Carnatic, and the grant confirmed by the Moghul Emperor in 1765.

Under the date July 2nd, 1702, the following instructive entry occurs in the Company's Stock books :—"Fort St. George, with the castle and fortifications, and territory thereto belonging, upon which a large city is built consisting of houses, which are held of, and pay rent to the said Governor and Company, together with the said city and its dependencies."

WARS AND RUMOURS OF WAR.

During the eighteenth century Fort St. George experienced many vicissitudes of fortune. Manucci describes an ill-omened comet visible at Madras early in 1702. It was noted in February. After a few days the star disappeared, but two tails were seen pointing southwards until March. "Such signs," he remarks, "have ever been the harbingers of approaching calamity, or some revolution among men."

In the same year Daud Khan, the Moghul Governor, quartered his troops at San Thomé and proceeded to invest Fort St. George. The sinister rumour spread abroad that Aurangzib had commanded the English stronghold to be razed to the ground. Fortunately nothing serious happened. Diplomacy won the day. A judicious distribution of money and other gifts led to the enemy withdrawing. The incident, however, served as a warning, and shortly afterwards a gunpowder factory was started in Madras. It was situated on the Island, to south-west of the Fort.

His long connection with the Moghul Court, coupled with the fact that he was a remarkably good linguist, led to Manucci being frequently employed, by the Governor of Fort St. George, in negotiations with neighbouring powers. On one such occasion he arranged a meeting between Daud Khan and Governor Pitt. Guided by Manucci the Moghul official set out from San Thomé with an escort of fifty horse. Midway he was met by the Madras Council. The town walls and those of the Inner Fort were found to be strongly manned. A guard of European and Indian soldiers lined the route from the main gate to that of the citadel. As Daud Khan approached, the troops began to execute a series of manoeuvres. This greatly alarmed Daud Khan, who imagined that he was about to be made a prisoner. At this juncture Governor Pitt appeared, followed by an imposing suite of officials and servants. He led his distinguished guest to his private apartments, which Manucci describes as magnificently furnished. Here

Governor Pitt presented Daud Khan with a gold chain and splendid pendant of ambergris and gold. Daud Khan was most desirous of possessing an embroidered Chinese quilt, which he saw on Pitt's bed. The latter promptly gave him two and offered him the entire bed. Thereafter the Governor drank Aurangzib's health to a salute of thirty-one guns. Daud Khan responded by toasting the King of England, when a similar salute was fired. Further toasts followed, each emphasised by an appropriate salute. After he had accepted several cases of wine and spirits, Daud Khan was entertained at a sumptuous banquet. The dining hall was decorated with a fine display of arms. Upon his requesting a spear, two were at once given to him. Having feasted, he lay down to rest for an hour and then took his leave. Governor Pitt accompanied him to the main gate. Here, at Daud Khan's special request, a final salve of guns was fired in his honour. A company of English musketeers gave him safe conduct to the bounds of San Thomé.

Shortly after Daud Khan succeeded Zulfikar Khan in 1701, as Nawab of the Carnatic, he made the Company a grant of the villages of Nungumbaukum, Vyasarpaudy, Trivettore, Shattancaud and Cuttiwaukum, now commonly known as Ennore.

The autumn of 1721 witnessed considerable destruction of property owing to a severe cyclone. Bridges were carried away and much damage done to shipping. Disputes with the French led the Governor of Pondicherry to prohibit the import of English goods. A force of Marathas appeared before Madras in 1741 and demanded tribute. The guns opened fire on them and they retreated.

FALL OF FORT ST. GEORGE.

Upon war breaking out between England and France de la Bourdonnais, Governor of Mauritius, collected a scratch fleet and set sail for Madras, where he appeared early in September 1746. By this time the settlement had attained considerable importance. The population exceeded two hundred and fifty thousand. The town itself consisted of three distinct divisions. To the south lay Fort St. George, or White Town surrounded by a wall with bastions at the corners. In addition to the large central edifice, where the Governor and other civil servants resided, it contained warehouses, public buildings, two churches and over a hundred private dwellings. It was essentially the European quarter. Including the garrison the inhabitants numbered three hundred. Immediately to north lay Black Town, also encircled by weak ramparts. It contained some handsome houses erected by wealthy Indians and Armenians, also several belonging to private European merchants engaged in trade on their own account, independent of the Company. The rest of the area consisted of bazaars and smaller houses. Outside the walls there was an extensive residential suburb stretching towards Kasimode. Several neighbouring villages and kuppams likewise looked to the Company's guns for protection.

On September 7th the invaders landed a strong force south of San Thomé. By the 8th they had erected a battery of five mortars and proceeded to an all-night bombardment of Fort St. George. Early on the following morning Governor Morse despatched two deputies to the French camp to treat. De la Bourdonnais insisted upon his right to dictate terms, whereupon they withdrew and the bombardment was resumed. The threat of a general attack made Governor Morse realise the futility of further resistance. Accordingly, he agreed to surrender, provided that de la Bourdonnais would undertake to restore the place upon payment of a ransom. As a result, the terms of capitulation were signed on September 10th, 1646. Thereafter de la Bourdonnais presented himself at the main gate of Fort St. George, supported by a large body of troops. He was met by the English Governor who handed over the keys. Subsequently de la Bourdonnais consented to accept a ransom of eleven lakhs of pagodas, otherwise forty-four lakhs of rupees. He then withdrew from Madras. Dupleix repudiated the agreement entered into by de la Bourdonnais. Fort St. George was garrisoned with twelve hundred French soldiers under command of a Swiss Captain named Paradis, about whom Ananda Ranga Pillai, Dubash to the French Governor of Pondicherry, has much to say in his celebrated Diary.

Governor Morse and the principal inhabitants were declared prisoners of war, and interned at Pondicherry. Some of the Company's servants' and a number of the garrison effected their escape from Madras, and made their way to the English factory at Fort St. David. Among the former was young Robert Clive, aged twenty, who had come out to India as a writer in the previous year and who, friendless, home-sick and in debt, had attempted to take his life soon after arrival at Fort St. George.

FORT ST. DAVID.

On the fall of Madras, Fort St. David, in South Arcot, was declared chief of the Company's factories on the East Coast. Originally known as Tegnapatam it had been sold to the traders for thirty thousand pagodas in 1690, by Ram Raja, son of the famous Maratha sovereign, Sivaji. The firman transferring the property to the Company specified the handing ever of "the Fort of Tegnapatam, with all its guns, buildings, etc . . . . as also all the grounds, woods and rivers round the said Fort within the random shot of a great gun." Governor Elihu Yale promptly despatched the "Defense, "with the "best piece of brass ordnance" that Madras possessed. This was fired by Gunner Brewster, on September 23rd, 1690. The range was excellent and took in "Cuddalore and its circumference, much beyond Tegnapatam and Mangee Kuppam."

Immediately upon possession, Yale re-named the stronghold in honour of the patron saint of Wales, inspired, probably, by the fact that he was born in Denbighshire. It is likewise pointed out that both his father and only son were called David.

Fort St. David continued to be the Company's principal factory and seat of Government until 1752, when Madras was restored to its old position. Finally, on June 2nd, 1758, Fort St. David surrendered to the French, under Lally, by whose orders it was razed to the ground.

MADRAS AGAIN BESIEGED.

The treaty of Aix-la-Chapelle gave Madras back to the English. As a precautionary measure the Company's servants lost no time in making themselves masters of San Thomé. Nevertheless the years that followed were anxious ones. Gradually Portuguese and Dutch competition slackened. The struggle for commercial and political supremacy resolved itself into a duel between the French and English. Matters reached a critical stage when, on December 12th, 1758, Lally threatened Fort St. George and actually occupied Black Town. Colonels Stringer-Lawrence and Draper put up an obstinate defence, holding out until February

17th, 1759, when the advent of a British fleet, under Admiral Pococke, caused the French to withdraw. Since that date Madras, although threatened, continued immune from actual attack until the recent world war. On the night of September 22nd, 1914, the German battle cruiser "Emden," commanded by the famous Captain von Müller, bombarded the coast, setting fire to an oil tank near the harbour, and breaching the outer wall of the High Court.

THE TREATY OF PARIS.

A temporary lull in hostilities followed the signing of the treaty of Paris in February, 1763. Pondicherry was restored, together with all French territories seized since 1749. In return, the French agreed not to erect warehouses, or despatch troops to Bengal. They renounced further territorial acquisitions in Orissa, and along the Coromandel Coast. Finally, they agreed to recognise Muhammad Ali Khan as Nawab of the Carnatic. The latter had already signified his gratitude to the Company for espousing his cause by ceding them the town of Poonamallee, fourteen miles south-west of Madras, and other lands dependant upon the Subah of Arcot. In 1763 he made them an additional grant of the major part of Chingleput district.

War between France and England again broke out in 1778 and persisted for five years. Sir Hector Munro seized Pondicherry. Meanwhile Madras continued to progress. The Board of Revenue was instituted in 1786. Orphanages were opened for soldiers' children. On December 12th, 1790, the Governor-General, Lord Cornwallis, arrived at Fort St. George, to personally command the force operating against Tippu Sultan, son of Haider Ali, the celebrated soldier of fortune, who had usurped the Government of Mysore. Two years later the Madras

Observatory was founded. In 1794 a squadron sailed from Madras to capture the Dutch settlements in Ceylon. Malacca, Bandra, and Amboyna. The Cape of Good Hope alse fell to the English. In 1795 Madras lighthouse was erected on the roof of the Exchange, now the British Infantry Mess in the Fort.

FINAL CAMPAIGN AGAINST TIPPU SULTAN.

The fact that Tippu Sultan had despatched an embassy from Seringapatam to the French Governor of Mauritius was regarded as a hostile act by the Governor-General, Lord Mornington, better known by his subsequent title of Marquis of Wellesley. The newly appointed Governor-General arrived at Fort St. George on April 29th, 1796. After a brief consultation with the authorities he proceeded to Calcutta, leaving instructions for the army to assemble at Madras. In August of the same year Lord Clive succeeded Lord Hobart as Governor of the senior presidency. A campaign against Tippu Sultan being decided upon, hostilities culminated with the siege of Seringapatam, by the Madras army under General Harris, supported by the Company's ally, the Nizam of Hyderabad. The investment commenced on April 5th, 1799. On the 14th General Stuart joined up with a strong force from Bombay. The capital was carried on May 4th, when Tippu Sultan was shot dead outside the Water Gate, by a grenadier ignorant of his identity.

Colonel Arthur Wellesley of the Madras Army, afterwards the famous Duke of Wellington, victor of Waterloo, was appointed to the military command of Seringapatam. The Hindu dynasty of Mysore was restored in the person of Krishna Raja Wodeyar. In the treaty which followed, between the Nizam of Hyderabad, the Peshwa of Poona and the Company, the English received considerable territorial concessions, which included the Nilgiris, and the greater share of Tanjore.

THE TREATY OF AMIENS.

Under the treaty of Amiens Pondicherry was restored to the French in 1801. That same year witnessed the establishment of the Supreme Court of Madras. The peace with France was of brief duration. In September 1803 Pondicherry was again taken by the Company's troops. A canal was opened connecting Madras and Ennore, and a treaty concluded with Mysore whereby the Company secured substantial additions of territory. In 1808 serious disaffection broke out in the Madras Army when Lord Bentinck and Colonel John Munro, Q. M. G., sanctioned Sir John Craddock's proposal to abolish the Tent contract, an allowance entitling Officers to supply tents for their men. As a result General Macdowell, Commander-in-Chief of the Madras forces, was ordered to England and perished at sea. Lord Minto came down to Madras to investigate the matter. Four of the insubordinate officers were cashiered. The remainder were given the option of standing their Court Martial, or of being dismissed the service. An exception was made in the case of those at Hyderabad, who were pardoned unconditionally.

CHANGES AND DEVELOPMENTS.

An Act of Parliament, passed in July 1813, renewed the Company's privileges for a period of twenty years. Simultaneously a distinction was drawn between territorial and commercial issues. Confusion of the two was no longer admitted. Furthermore, trade with India ceased to be a monopoly, but was declared open to all British subjects. Alone in China did the Company retain their exclusive prerogative. King George III asserted his sovereign right by nominating a Bishop of India, and an Archdeacon to each presidency. Their stipends were made a charge upon the Company.

In June 1834 Lord Macaulay arrived in Madras as a legal member of the Supreme Court of Calcutta. His famous Penal Code came into operation on New Year's Day, 1862. The Madras Chamber of Commerce was established in 1836. Four years later the Madras Army despatched a contingent to China. The Officers of the 37th Madras Infantry were lost at sea in the wreck of the "Golcondah," nevertheless the battalion gained such signal distinction in the campaign as to be raised to the rank of a Grenadier Regiment. In April of the following year Lord Elphinstone opened Madras University in College Hall. Eighteen months later Black Town was almost entirely burnt down. December 1842 was noteworthy by reason of the arrival of the *Hindustan*, the first steamer launched by the Peninsular and Oriental Company. The railway works date from June 9th, 1853. Just twelve months later the earliest locomotive for Madras was landed. Ultimately the railway line was opened for traffic in 1856. The following autumn was memorable for the appointment of eighteen uncovenanted deputy collectors of Madras, and the establishment of the Forest Conservancy Department. Another step forward was the inauguration of a normal school.

PASSING OF THE OLD ORDER.

Although Madras escaped the ill effects of the sepoy mutiny in 1857, the city participated in the sweeping changes which followed. All the territories owned by the Honourable East India Company, either by virtue of treaty, purchase or conquest, were declared vested in Queen Victoria, in whose name the Government was thenceforward conducted.

The trader's task was accomplished. They had built up an Empire. All the while they had imagined themselves humble factors. Ill paid and practically left to fend for themselves by their employers, in whose eyes they were eternally suspect, they had been unconsciously working out a great and mysterious destiny.

Possibly some day a gifted sculptor will typify the birth of the British Indian Empire. In the centre a globe. To west of it Queen Elizabeth signing the charter incorporating the Honourable East India Company. On the opposite side the Maharaja of Vijianagar sanctioning the gold-plated kaul conveying Madras to the merchants. At the feet of the two sovereigns the sculptor might well place an English trader of the seventeenth century, yard measure in hand, and an Indian weaver delivering the stipulated length of stamped calico.

MUNICIPAL DIVISIONS.

At present Madras contains twenty divisions. The Legislative Council have passed a new Municipal Bill increasing this number to thirty.

Photo by Lt.-Col. H. A. Newell.

EAST ENTRANCE TO FORT ST. GEORGE.

ITINERARY.

FIRST DAY..............*Morning*.

VISIT FORT ST. GEORGE, HIGH COURT, LAW COLLEGE AND THE HARBOUR.

FORT ST. GEORGE.

Girdled by low khaki coloured walls, and the remains of a moat, Fort St. George would seem to shun rather than court attention, were it not for the tall spire of St. Mary's Church, which kindly time has mellowed to the soft tint of old ivory, and the lofty flagstaff dominating the great central redan of the sea face.

The most frequented entrance is St. George's Gate, in the northern part of the west wall. It leads into Poonamallee High Road and George Town. Lower down, on the same side to south, Wallajah Gate and Ravelin open into Mount Road, a splendid thoroughfare completed in 1795, that runs out to St. Thomas' Mount, a distance of eight miles. A branch of the Cooum River skirts the western defences. Inside the ramparts their course is traced by a straight broad walk known as Outer Curtain Street. This meets San Thomé Street, underlying the south wall. Midway is San Thomé Gate, its approach guarded by a traverse of mud and bricks neatly faced with cut stone. Here the moat has been filled in. Glimpses of the Station Hospital are visible through an intervening screen of trees.

The east wall commands the sea which, prior to the construction of the harbour, came very much nearer than at present. At one time the waves actually washed away part of the fortifications. So serious was the menace that, in 1762, the Court of Directors expressed the fear that it would be impossible to devise any means whereby their stronghold might be saved from the encroachments of the Bay of Bengal.

A massive redan, surmounted by a flagstaff said to be the highest in India, occupies the centre of the east curtain. Flanking it are the North and South Sea Gates. These are supplemented by two modern park gates of wrought iron erected in honour of the Council Chamber.

They stand apart from the fortifications and are strangely incongruous. Tradition avers that the then Governor considered the existing entrances too low and insignificant for the passage of exalted personages. When he expressed this opinion to the General the latter retorted, so says the anecdote :—" Better men went out through those old gates than will ever come in by the new ones."

The original flagstaff stood in the south-east bastion of the first Fort St. George built by Day and Cogan. This bastion was the earliest erected and received the name of English Point. The present flagstaff is believed to have replaced the mast of the French frigate "La Forte," captured by the "Sybil" in 1792, and blown down about half a century ago, when the naval authorities at Trincomallee erected the existing one.

Outside the sea wall is a moat. Grass grows at the bottom and the sides are lined with stone. Parallel with it Beach Road runs northward towards the harbour. Beyond again stretches a wide expanse of yellow sand, hot and shadeless but for a few wind-swept casuarina trees. A white line of restless surf divides the flat beach from a sea of a clear bright blue, excepting when the threat of rain turns it an almost equally vivid green.

Here it was, on the sandy foreshore, that the Company's merchants assembled to traffic with the sailing ships riding at an anchor in the roadstead. English vessels were distinguished by the Company's flag, horizontal red lines on a white ground. The Sea Gate served as Exchange, where business men of various nationalities met daily at 11 A.M.

Doctor Fryer, Surgeon to the Company, visited Madras in July 1673. He writes :—" I went ashore in a musoola boat, wherein ten men paddle, the two aftermost of whom are the steersmen, using their paddles instead of a rudder . . . . . . Though we landed wet the sand was scalding hot, which made me recollect my steps and hasten to the Fort. As it looked on the water it appeared a place of good force. The outwork is walled with stone a good height, thick enough to blunt a cannon ball kept by a dozen ordnance at each side the water gate, besides a half moon of five guns."

Following York Road, as it proceeds northward under the east wall inside the Fort, the Station Mess is passed on the left. It is a big three-storied yellow building characterised by green woodwork and a white pillared verandah. Originally the private residence of a Mr. Hughes, the site was purchased for the erection of an Exchange at the instigation of Peter Cassey Massin who, in 1787, drew the attention of Government to the inadequate accommodation provided in Pitt's old colonnade by the Sea Gate. A sum was consequently raised by public lotteries, and the work undertaken by a Company possessing a capital of pagodas 25,000 in twenty-five shares. The ground floor was devoted to warehouses and offices. Above was the Exchange, free to all merchants, dealers, commanders of ships or others having any concern in trade. It likewise contained a coffee room, a broker's office and a committee room. The walls of the Exchange were hung with portraits of Cornwallis, Coote, General Meadows, Lord Wellesley, the Duke of Wellington and others. Public meetings, lottery drawings and entertainments were also held there. Auction rooms, where Tippu Sultan's crown jewels were auctioned in 1802, a subscription library and the Madras Bank were situated on the ground floor. In 1826 the Government rented the Exchange for public offices. Prior to that the roof had, as early as 1795, served as a base for the lighthouse, seemingly an iron framed structure supporting a lantern, reflectors and twelve lamps fed with cocoanut oil. From 1861 downwards the old Exchange building has been used as the Officers' Mess of the British regiment stationed in the Fort. It was purchased from the shareholders in 1882, since when it has remained Government property.

The North East Demi-Bastion marks the corner, whence it commands the sea, and the six tall posts of the wireless station erected on slightly rising ground, to north of the ramparts, on the site of old Black Town. An inclined way leads to the top of the battlements. A sentry on guard bars the ascent to all unprovided with a pass. Further to west is the Orillon Demi-Bastion, and, finally, the Mint Bastion in the north-west angle.

Wide streets and cross roads traverse the enclosure. The mellow colouring of the old buildings is refreshingly blended with the occasional green of trees, chiefly asoka, tamarind, palm and croton. Here are no ruined structures, no oppressive burden of years, the silence and decay of a city that had its day many centuries ago, but rather the peaceful contentment of prosperous and honoured middle age.

Fort St. George is a classic. The memories which it evokes, however, are warm and living. Its heroes belong to modern, not ancient history. The earth rests lightly upon them. They quicken at a touch. Pitt, Coote, Clive, Charnock, Stringer-Lawrence, Munro are still names to conjure with, and their descendants are with us yet.

FIRST FORT.

When planning their Fort Cogan and Day were chiefly inspired by utilitarian and economic motives, hence they limited themselves to essentials, and were content to follow the square form common at that period. The Naik's grant entitled them to build "in or about Madraspatam," and also to appropriate the revenues of that place for two years, from which it would appear that they received all the land within its boundaries. Approximately the tract extended three and a quarter miles from north to south, its mean width being about a mile. This they held as a fief from the Naik, and enclosed with a boundary hedge of cactus and aloes.

Work began on March 1st, 1640, with the erection of the Factory or Castle, a plain box-like edifice, three stories high, without verandah or external ornament. A parapet encircled the flat roof which, quaintly enough, was surmounted by a dome. The ground floor was devoted to warehouses. Above was the Consultation Room, as the Council Chamber was styled. The Agent's quarters were on the top floor. Other apartments included a general dining-room, where all messed together, and lodgings for the Company's merchants, factors, writers and apprentices,

The building was diagonally placed in a paved quadrangle enclosed by battlemented walls. Each of its four faces commanded a corner bastion. The first of these turrets was English Point, in the south-east angle. It was finished in 1640, when eight iron guns were mounted and the flagstaff, which flew the Royal Standard. The north-east bastion was ready in 1641. A third, of earth, was put up a year later and faced with cut stone in 1643. Thereafter operations dragged. The fourth tower and one curtain took from 1644 until 1652. Then a sudden recrudescence of interest resulted in the Fort being pronounced finished in 1653.

The main gate faced west and was regarded as the front of the Factory. A small back-door communicated with the beach. The enclosed area measured about 60 yards square, the salient points of the bastions being some 100 yards apart. From the centre to the sea was a distance of 190 yards, whereas the river lay 110 yards away to the west. The civil establishment were allotted quarters in the Factory, and the garrison under the ramparts. Such was the original Fort St. George.

Soon European dwellings sprang up around, creating a settlement that came to be known as Christian, or White Town. This was defended by a fortified wall completed by Greenhill during his second term of office (1655-1659). Bastions were added and gates forming an outer fort of which Day and Cogan's was the citadel. The latter survived as such until 1714 when it was demolished and the site converted into the Fort square.

The outbreak of war with Holland forced the merchants to strengthen their defences in view of a probable attack from their Dutch neighbours. Writing on the subject to the Company in September 1654, President Baker, Agent Greenhill and others report:— "Our Fort is reduced to a very good posture to defend itself against any ordinary enemy had we but men of courage and resolution about us to keep it. But for the matter of accommodation it is in as poor a condition as may be, having neither good rooms for entertainment nor good chambers for lodging."

IMPROVEMENT.

Sir Edward Winter assumed office at Madras in the autumn of 1662. He promptly set about enlarging the Factory and improving the station generally. More warehouses were erected. Adequate quarters were assigned to the Chaplain, and civil servants, in the main building, to which a chapel was added and a library. The garrison was reinforced by forty-five English soldiers. Winter reported what he had effected to the Court of Directors in the following terms :—"The Mansion House is very noble, wherein may constantly abide the Agent, Second, Third and Fourth. Besides a very beautiful chapel for Divine Service, and convenient lodging for the Minister, as also a fair dining room and cellar." Later on the Chapel likewise served as Court of Judicature. It was first put to this use on April 10th, 1678. Thereafter the Governor and his Council assembled in it regularly twice a week, namely on Wednesday and Saturday, to try cases by jury.

THE EARLIEST CHURCH.

The immunity from taxes promised by Day and Cogan, together with offers of free grants of land to settlers, induced a number of Portuguese to abandon San Thomé, and its fast declining trade, and establish themselves at Fort St. George. This led Father Ephraim de Nevers to found a Capuchin Mission at Madras, where, in 1642, he built the Catholic Church of St. Andrews immediately to the north of the Factory ramparts. Four years later the Reverend William Isaacson arrived at Fort St. George as Minister to the Protestant community, who do not appear to have had a regular piace of worship until Sir John Winter provided them with a chapel in 1662. In that same year San Thomé was captured by the Muhammadan army of Golcondah. This was followed by a general exodus of Portuguese to Madras. The Church of St. Andrews was found too small to accommodate the increased congregation. A very much larger bomb-proof edifice of the same name was erected on, or near, the original site. It was consecrated in 1675, when Sir William Langhorne caused a salute of guns to be fired, an action which appears to have excited hostile comment in some quarters. During the siege of 1746 it sheltered the women and children of the garrison and also served as hospital for the wounded. It was demolished in 1752.

FORT ST. GEORGE IN 1673.

Fryer's description of Fort St. George, as seen by him in 1673, is clear and graphic. He prefaces his account by telling how he was carried ashore on men's shoulders, the usual mode of landing from a musoola boat. The sea wall impressed him favourably. The corner bastions, respectively termed Fishing Point and St. Thomas Point, each mounted twelve guns. From them two lines of stout wooden palisadoes stretched to the water. The south side was protected by a moat as far as the Round Bastion, at the south-west angle, beyond which lay fields that were invariably flooded during the autumn rains. The west side was defenceless excepting for the river and the houses and gardens lining its banks. Calder's Point was the bastion guarding the north-west angle. It adjoined the curtain and parapet drawn along the northern face of Christian Town, here entered by Middle Gate and Choultry Gate. The interior of each doorway was guarded by two cannons, five more defending the rampart above.

The Inner Fort stood near the Sea Gate. It practically divided the enclosure into northern and southern halves. Its four square corner towers mounted forty guns, while the connecting curtains bristled with five and a half inch eighteen pounders. St. George's standard flew from the south-east angle. The main entrance was a high portico to west and opened into Choultry Street, flanked by the Guard Room, which daily turned out two hundred men for duty. Fryer estimates the garrison at seven hundred, including British soldiers, Portuguese and the Gun Room crew, a corps recruited from sailors. A broad paved walk to east connected the small postern at the back of the Inner Fort with the Sea Gate of the outer ramparts. Fryer describes the streets of White Town as "sweet and clean." They were of sand, the narrow side walks alone being brick paved. The houses were two storeys in height, nevertheless he extols them as possessing beautiful porticos, and terraced walks with shade trees planted before the doors. He alludes to the Portuguese Church of St. Andrews, near the northern rampart of the Inner Fort and describes the Outer Fort as oblong. As a matter of fact, it was quadrilateral, the northern face being much longer than the southern, while the west side followed the curve of the river.

Fryer speaks of the Governor, Sir William Langhorne, as "a gentleman of indefatigable industry and worth." He mentions his personal guard of between three and four hundred Indians, in addition to which a further force, some fifteen hundred strong, was ever within call. Sir Willian Langhorne invariably appeared in public with an imposing retinue swelled by his Council and Factors on horseback, and their ladies in curtained litters. Music was provided by fifes, drums and trumpets, and a flag was carried, the device of which was two white balls on a red ground. According to Fryer the English community numbered three hundred, and the Portuguese as many thousand.

FORTIFICATIONS.

By 1682 the sea had so far encroached as to cause the collapse of part of the east wall, including Langhorne's Bastion near St. Thomas Point. The damage was made good. Orders were received to replace the mud ramparts of Black Town with a masonry wall. Double doors were provided at all the sally ports on the river side of the Fort, and powder was stored in godowns under the curtain adjoining St. Thomas Point.

The accession of James II was solemnised with much ceremony in 1685. Two years afterwards word was received to curtail the amount of powder lavished upon salutes. On sighting the Fort, ships were henceforward to fire five guns only.

UNION JACK HOISTED.

Elihu Yale was appointed Governor in 1687. The Company expressed disapproval of their Fort flying St. George's standard, and required it to be replaced by the Union Jack. The latter was accordingly hoisted on June 12th, 1688, in the presence of the assembled military and civil personnel. The Governor solemnly drank the King's health, while the ships in the roadstead, and the guns of the garrison thundered a royal salute. Afterwards a reception was held on the terrace of the citadel. Prisoners were liberated. The poor were fed and punch was served out freely to the troops.

Yale effected some marked improvements and suggested others, which were eventually executed long after his time. He strengthened the defences of Black Town by rebuilding the ramparts and erecting the bastion known as Queen's Point, at the junction of the river and the drainage canal. He substituted regular names for the different parts of the Fort. Previously these had been loosely designated by a variety of titles, a confusing practice likely to have disastrous results in the event of hostile attack, when safety would depend upon orders being instantly understood and obeyed.

At that epoch White Town contained a hundred and twenty-eight private dwellings, half of which were inhabited by Portuguese, who paid no rent, but who took their turn at mounting guard. There were seven main streets. Narrow lanes ran under the curtains. Yale appears to have resided in a house built by Sir Edward Winter in Middle Street. The fashionable suburb was Peddanaikapetta, where all who could afford it laid out pleasure grounds, planted fruit trees and flowers and built those Garden Houses for which old Madras was famous. It was in this quarter that Yale assigned a tract to weavers, and thereby drew many fresh settlers to Madras. Yale was succeeded by Higginson in 1692. The new Governor found the old Factory House in so tumble-down a state that he decided to demolish it and build afresh. He removed to Jearsey House, Charles Street, in 1693, whither the general dining table was temporarily transferred.

Photo by Wiele & Klein.

THE OLD FORT HOUSE, NOW THE SECRETARIAT & ST. MARY'S CHURCH, FORT ST. GEORGE.

TH E SECRETARIAT.

The plan sanctioned by Higginson differed essentially from that of Day and Cogan. Instead of being square and diagonally placed the second Fort House measured 110 feet by 55 feet, its two faces being parallel with the corresponding curtains of the citadel. These dimensions were preserved until 1825 when wings were added at either end. The interior was converted into Government offices, and still serves this purpose under the name of the Secretariat, a yellow building fronting westward, the central portion of which dates from 1694.

ST. MARY'S CHURCH.

No sooner was Streynsham Master appointed Governor than he started to raise a public subscription for the purpose of building a Protestant Church. He himself headed the list with pagodas 100. A site was selected under the southern curtain of the Inner Fort, and a plan approved wherein it was laid down that the sacred edifice should be 80 feet long, 56 feet broad within the walls, and built with three aisles arched with brick and stone.

When pagodas 805 had been contributed the work began on March 25th, 1678. It was completed two and a half years later, and can claim the distinction of being the oldest masonry structure in the Fort. The north curtain and north-east bastion date from about the same time. A commission was sent out to the Governor by the Lord Bishop of London sanctioning the dedication service, which was followed by the usual firing of cannon accompanied by volleys of small shot. Mr. Richard Portman was the first minister. The architect is believed to have been William Dixon, the Chief Gunner, to whom the task would naturally have been allotted. From a plan dated 1760 the internal dimensions were 64 feet by 56 feet. The sanctuary to the east, and the recess under the gallery at the west end increased the length to 86 feet. An organ was installed in 1687, having been purchased for pagodas 70 from Captain Weldten of the ship 'Curtana.' Five years later the Company intimated their intention of sending out a peal of six bells. In 1693 a seat was set apart for the Mayor below the clerk's desk. Due provision was made for a silver gilt mace to be prominently displayed at either side of him. A place near by was allotted for his wife. The Governor and his Council did not mingle with the congregation. They sat apart in the small gallery at the back. At the Governor's entrance the organ immediately struck up. Service was at 7 A.M. Full dress, according to the European mode of the period, was *de rigeur*, and wigs were worn, so that the heat was intolerable. A writer describes the sufferings which this vogue involved by saying :—" Every time a man visited the Church he lost some ounces by perspiration."

In 1692 a weekly service was instituted for Portuguese Protestants, and conducted by a chaplain familiar with their language.

THE BELFRY.

As was the architectural custom of the period the belfry was detached. A narrow passage divided it from the main building to which it was subsequently joined in 1760. The tower was finished in 1701 and the steeple added nine years later. When the French forces, under Lally, besieged Madras in 1758, it served as a look-out post, and sustained such damage that it was found necessary to demolish it in 1767. In 1795 a proposal was advanced to utilise it as a light-house. The Government approved the scheme which was, however, rejected by the chaplains, who based their objection on the original engagement entered into in 1680, that the Church should never serve any secular purpose. The steeple was re-built in 1795.

In spite of the proviso cited by the Chaplains St. Mary's had more than once been utilised for military purposes. When the French took Madras in 1746 they employed the Church as a reservoir for fresh water. The autumn of 1758 witnessed its conversion into a British barracks, where a hundred and fifty men were quartered. Bales of cotton were piled on the bomb-proof roof. During the war with Haider Ali it was used as a granary in 1782, owing to the necessity for storing large reserves of foodstuffs in Fort St. George. Meanwhile divine service was held in the great hall of Admiralty House near by. This famous building was in Charles Street. It is now the Accountant General's Office.

CHURCHYARD.

An iron railing encloses the narrow churchyard. To north the ground is paved with closely set gravestones. Most of the deeply cut inscriptions are in Latin. The majority display elaborately engraved coats of arms intermingled th skulls and cross bones, a favourite form of sepulchral decoration in the seventeenth and eighteenth centuries. A few were removed from the Capuchin Church of St. Andrews, demolished, by the Company's orders, in 1752. The others came from the old English burial ground in Black Town, the site of which is now covered by the Law College and adjacent tennis courts. The immense monuments, of which they formed part, afforded valuable cover to Lally's troops in 1758-59 during the siege of Fort St. George. Military considerations led to their subsequently being razed to the ground, the inscribed portions being preserved in their present form. In each case the stone is gneiss quarried at Pallaveram. The oldest is that to the memory of President Aaron Baker's wife, who died at sea in 1662 on her voyage to Madras. It was broken in transit and the fragments pieced together. Another commemorates Thomas Clarke who, in 1641, built the first private house in the English settlement at Madras. It stood north-west of Day and Cogan's Fort, outside the fortified wall subsequently built around White Town. When a Dutch attack was feared in 1673, it was cleared away to make room for the bastion known as Caldera Point. Later on Clarke, who was son of a former agent at Masulipatam, planned a garden, and erected a house in Muthialpetta, at the southern end of what is now Popham's Broadway. He died on October 4th, 1683, and was interred in St. Andrews, White Town. His widow married Manucci, the Venetian physician world famed as the author of the "Storia do Mogor," hence his house in Popham's Broadway figures on old maps as Manucci's Garden. His name long survived in connection with Clarke's Gate, one of the principal ports of Black Town.

During the war with Haider Ali in 1782 some of the tombstones are said to have served as gun platforms.

THE INTERIOR.

The interior of the Church is whitewashed. Raised rose ornaments stand out in white relief from the vaulted grey ceiling. Little is visible of the walls, which are covered with handsome marble tablets of much historical interest. Entering by the side door, near the south-west corner, the eye is first caught by a life-sized statue of Lieut.-Colonel Hercules Pepper, of the 34th Light Infantry, who died in Fort St. George on July 25th, 1826. Near by is a little black stone font surmounted by a pyramidal cover of elaborately carved teak-wood. A few steps further on a recess in the end wall contains a small upper gallery conspicuous for a beautiful and curious wooden screen, the design of which introduces pelicans. This was where the Governor sat. Below, and almost hidden from sight behind a pew, is a rather gloomy grey monument to Lady Hobart and her infant son, who died on August 7th, 1796. In close proximity is a fine monument, by Flaxman, to Gericke, the noted Danish Missionary, obit 1804. Another, by the same celebrated sculptor, commemorates Josiah Webbe. A third wall tablet, by Flaxman, was erected by the Company in 1807 to Frederick Christian Swartz, the famous missionary to whom the dying Raja of Tanjore confided the regency of his country, and the guardianship of his adopted son. The neighbouring corner holds a life-size statue, by Turnouth, of Brigadier-General Conway, popularly known as the "Soldiers' Friend." He long served as Adjutant-General and died of cholera at Guntoor in 1837. Conway's Gardens, Kilpauk, became his property in 1816. Government purchased the estate in 1838 and utilised it first as a Female Asylum and afterwards as an Orphanage. On the floor near the statue a gravestone bears the name of Lieut.-General Sir John Doveton and the date, November 7th, 1847. The wall above displays the colours of the 102nd Royal Madras Fusiliers, now the Royal Dublin Fusiliers. A second floor tablet is to Major-General Sir Thomas Munro, Governor of Madras, who died on July 6th, 1827. The fine equestrian statue of him near the parade ground, Mount Road, is the handsomest in the city. Particular interest attaches to the plain gravestone, to the right of the chancel, inscribed "In Memoriam." It marks the resting place of Lord Pigot, the first man to be buried in St. Mary's Church. Appointed Governor for the second time in 1775, Lord Pigot was arrested by order of his own Council in the following year, and kept a prisoner at St. Thomas Mount until 1777, when he was brought back to Madras and confined in the Governor's Garden House, where he died on May 11th. Neither name nor date marked his burial place. Excavations under the chancel in 1874 uncovered a vault containing a nameless coffin. The Duke of Buckingham was Governor at the time. He assumed the sepulchre to be that of Lord Pigot and ordered a plain floor tablet to be placed over the spot.

ALTAR PIECE.

Much controversy has been excited by the beautiful oil painting of "The Lord's Supper" above the communion table. It is believed to be the work of a pupil of Raphael, the chalice having been painted by the master's own hand. The general opinion is that the picture formed part of the spoils taken at the second capture of Pondicherry by the British. This theory is supported by the fact that it first figures in the Vestry records in 1782. Salmon, who visited Fort St. George in 1699, mentions "a handsome altar piece," in the English Church, as he styles St. Mary's. This was probably of carved woodwork. Protestant prejudice at that period was strongly against pictures in places of worship.

THE ORGAN.

The organ is to the left of the chancel. A brass tablet bears the following inscription :—"This organ, the property of Captain John Hay, Military Secretary to the Right Honourable Lord Harris, was presented to St. Mary's Church, Fort St. George, by Sir Adam Hay, Bart., father of the deceased. . Erected January 1859 in lieu of one presented by John Smith, Esq., A. D. 1760.

Below, a second inscription states that the above was superseded by the present organ installed in 1894 to the memory of those who died for duty in India, and more particularly such as were buried in the Church. Funds for the purpose were collected by the Rev. A. C. Taylor, assisted by the Rev. C. H. Pelly, Garrison Chaplains. The tablet was erected by the Rev. Frank Penny, L.L.M., Senior Chaplain, His Majesty's Indian Service, 1891.

The original organ, purchased from Captain Weldten in 1687, was removed to Pondicherry by the French in 1746, after the capture of Fort St. George. Madras was restored to the English in 1749. Two years later an order was sent to England wherein Mr. Bridges was instructed to supply a new organ to cost £300. The old one was recovered in 1761 after Pondicherry had yielded to the English. When, in 1782, the Church was used as a granary, the organ was removed, and sustained damages in the process, for which compensation was claimed, but refused on the ground that too long a time had elapsed before advancing the claim.

CHURCH RECORDS.

Application to view the Church Records and silver plate should be made in advance to the Chaplain. The registers are of considerable historical value and date from October 28th, 1680. The first volume is a parchment copy made in 1739 by Alexander Wynch, at that time a writer in the Company's service, and afterwards Governor of Fort St. George from 1773 until 1775. The earliest marriage entry is that of Governor Elihu Yale, with Catherine, widow of Joseph Hynmers. They had one son, David, who died, when three years of age, and was buried in Black Town. His tomb is a remarkable monument and stands at the back of the Law College where it immediately attracts attention. Elihu Yale is best remembered in connection with the famous University named after him in the United States. He was born at New Haven, Connecticut, in North America on April 5th, 1648, His father, David Yale, was a native of Wrexham, Denbighshire, to which place he returned from America when his son, Elihu, was four years old. The latter came out to India in 1672. Upon his retirement, in 1699, he resided at Plas Grono, near Wrexham, in a house that had belonged to his father. In 1718 Cotton Mather requested Yale to assist the struggling collegiate school of Connecticut with a gift of books and pictures. The ex-Governor of Madras responded with a generous supply valued at £560. In gratitude for the donation the school, and finally the famous University, came to bear his name.

Yet another interesting entry records the baptism of three daughters of Job Charnock, the founder of Calcutta, by a Hindu lady whom he had rescued from the flames of satti. A third is the marriage of the famous Lord Clive, afterwards victor of Plassey who, on February 18th, 1753, was united to Margaret Maskelyne.

SILVER PLATE.

In 1687 Governor Elihu Yale presented St. Mary's Church with a massive silver alms dish of plain design but for the bevelled rim, and a deeply embossed coat of arms, his own. A larger alms dish, of similar pattern, but less admirable workmanship, was donated by Lady Goldsborough, wife of Sir John Goldsborough. The latter was a trusted commander in the Company's fleet. Accompanied by his wife and children, he arrived at Fort St. George in December 1692, charged with the mission of settling the dispute between Governor Yale and the Mayor's Court. In the following July he set sail for Bengal, where he died suddenly. Sir John Goldsborough was succeeded by Sir John Gayer. Lady Goldsborough continued to reside in Madras. She occupied Jearsey House, Charles

Street, in Fort St. George until the premises were required for public purposes. Thereafter the Company allotted her apartments in their Garden House. In 1695 she married Mr. Roger Braddyl of the Civil Service.

Another interesting relic is a Bible, printed in 1660, which belonged to Governor Streynsham Master (1677-81) by whose exertions St. Mary's Church was built. It was presented in 1881 by his descendant, Mr. C. G. Master, M.C.S.

CHAPLAIN'S QUARTERS.

These are situated at the southern end of St. Thomas Street, in the last house on the west side. Originally the Church House, as it was styled, adjoined St. Mary's, which it separated from the Hospital built by public subscription in 1679 and subsequently acquired by the Company as quarters for their civil staff. While it served the latter capacity it was known as the College. This in turn was converted into the Export warehouse. The Town Hall stood on the east side of St. Thomas Street almost opposite St. Mary's Church. In the early days of the settlement the thoroughfare was the route invariably followed by Muckwa funerals proceeding from the neighbouring fishing village to the Portuguese Church.

ACCOUNTANT-GENERAL'S OFFICE.

To south of St. Mary's Church a dignified old yellow building picked out with white, asserts itself on the further side of Charles Street. This is none other than Admiralty House, its fame, historical significance and its identity concealed under the alias of Accountant-General's Office. The property belonged to Coja Nazar Jacob Jan, an Armenian, who settled in Madras in 1702. He willed it to Coja Sultan David, in whose time it was known as the Great House, Charles Street. In 1749 David's son, Shamier, was notified by Stringer-Lawrence that the Company contemplated buying the mansion, and two large godowns appertaining thereto. In November of the same year it became the official residence of the acting Deputy Governor, Mr. Richard Prince, at a rental of pagodas 30 per mensem. Afterwards it appears to have reverted to Shamier, from whom it was leased by Robert Clive and others. The order evicting Armenians from White Town compelled Shamier to dispose of it. Apparently he sold it to a Portuguese named De Castro, from whom the Company

purchased it for pagodas 6,000. In 1755 permission was asked to assign a portion of it for the accommodation of visitors, particularly as considerable difficulty was experienced in providing Admiral Watson with suitable quarters in the Fort. It was further agreed that a Court of Admiralty should be established in it for the trial of mutineers.

In 1758 the building first figures in official registers as Admiralty House. During the French siege it served as a barracks for two hundred men. Three years later, namely in 1762, it was completely furnished for the reception of guests, and a housekeeper appointed. All the expenses were borne by the Company. Governor Josiah DuPre (1770-73) made it his town residence, and subsequent Governors followed his example. State receptions were held in it prior to the erection of the present Banqueting Hall, in 1802, intended by Edward, Lord Clive, as a memorial of the victories of Plassey and Seringapatam,

Hostilities with Haider Ali in 1782 led to over-crowding of the Fort owing to the influx of naval officers, and French and Dutch prisoners of war. St. Mary's Church was converted into a granary for eighteen months, during which time the Great Hall, Admiralty House, was consecrated to divine service. Extensive repairs were effected by Governor Sir Thomas Rumbold (1778-80) who, on arrival, reported both Government Houses, *i.e.*, Admiralty House, and the Garden House, as too small for the accommodation of his family. Nevertheless it was in Admiralty House that Sir John Lindsay had stayed in 1770, when he arrived in Madras as Naval Commander-in-Chief and Minister Plenipotentiary to the Court of the Nawab of the Carnatic, at Chepauk. The Governor-General, Lord Mornington, also lived in it during his sojourn in Madras in 1799. Under Edward, Lord Clive (1798-1803), it was the scene of many brilliant functions, until he decided upon its abandonment in 1800, and ordered its transfer to the Revenue Department.

FORT SQUARE.

The original Factory House, or Castle erected by Day and Cogan in 1640, had been re-built on an entirely different plan in 1695. This second edifice survives in the present Secretariat. The Fort itself remained standing until 1714, by which date one of the bastions had collapsed. Furthermore Governor Harrison (1709-1717) reported that the lodgings under the curtain, the armoury, gold mint, store-rooms and godowns were in a lamentable condition, and beyond repair. Such being the case, it was decided to demolish the old citadel and replace it with a strong walled enclosure adapted to civil requirements, which should bear the name of Fort Square. The plan sanctioned made due provision for housing all covenanted servants of the Company, who were required to be indoors by 10-30 P.M., at which hour the gates were shut. It also included the Gold Mint, Armoury, Treasury, Cook Room, and other offices. By June 1715 the walls of the square were 5 feet above ground. The work was finished about four years later at a cost of Pagodas 160,000 and survived until 1825, when it was cleared away. The transport of rubbish from the old Fort led to the construction of the first bridge across the river which, prior to 1714, had been traversed by boat. The main gate continued to be on the West side. It was surmounted by a cupola, and a clock made locally by a Frenchman for pagodas 60. On completion, the bell of the citadel was found too small for the clock, whereupon the church wardens offered that of St. Mary's. The Church bell proved suitable and was accepted.

Governor George Morton Pitt (1730-1735) constructed a handsome colonnade from the Fort Square to the Sea Gate. This was roofed over and lined with thirty-two pillars, ranged in four rows, of black Pallavaram gneiss. When the French captured Madras in 1746 they carried off the columns to Pondicherry. There they remained until 1761, in which year the British stormed the place, and restored the pillars to their former position in Pitt's Arcade. For a long time the Arcade constituted the Exchange. During the 19th century it was walled in at the sides and converted into a Government Press, and finally a Record Office. In 1910 Pitt's colonnade was sacrificed to the new Council Chamber, the exterior of which now displays twenty of the best preserved of the columns. During the brief French bombardment, in September 1746, the enemy concentrated their fire upon the Fort Square inhabited by the civil employees of the Company. This suggests the vexed question as to which house the famous Robert Clive was in when, as a youngster, newly arrived at Madras in 1745, he made the celebrated attempt on his life with a firearm that refused to go off. There can be little doubt but that the Fort Square was the scene of this historical incident.

To meet the requirements of the garrison it was decided to provide a bazaar in White Town. Accordingly in 1780 a row of thirty shops was erected along the east wall of Fort Square, facing the Sea Gate. To north lay Portuguese Square, once the site of St. Andrew's Church and the dwellings and offices of the priests. After the removal of these the ground was allotted for the accommodation of those Civil Servants who could not be lodged in Fort Square. The Armoury occupied the southern block of the latter until 1776, when it was divided up among eight public offices.

STATUE OF LORD CORNWALLIS.

After his victorious campaign against Tipu Sultan, Lord Cornwallis returned to Madras in 1792, where the two hostage princes, sons of the Mysore sovereign, were detained for over a year. A statue of Lord Cornwallis was publicly subscribed for and erected on the parade ground to west of the Fort Square in 1800. It was of white marble, executed by Thomas Banks, and depicts Lord Cornwallis, wearing peer's robes over military uniform. The carved pedestal portrays the surrender of Tipu Sultan's two sons as hostages. When the walls of the square were pulled down in 1825, the monument was moved eastward to a favourable position in view of the Secretariat, as the Fort House had come to be styled. It was placed in a round stone pavilion which still survives. About it were grouped brass cannon. These included a couple of Spanish guns taken at Manila and inscribed with the date 1604. Others were Danish, believed to have been handed over at the delivery of Tranquebar in 1801. Some, decorated with Tipu Sultan's tiger emblem, were brought from Seringapatam in 1799. Early in the 20th century the statue was transferred to the Reading Room of the Connemara Library in Pantheon Road. The cannon were deposited in the adjacent Museum.

THE COUNCIL CHAMBER.

This dates from 1910 and is a spacious white building adjoining the Secretariat to the east. The main entrance faces the Sea Gate and flag-staff. It admits to the Legislative Council Chamber, a large and handsome apartment paved with black and white marble, a wooden gallery at either end, white walls, wooden wainscotting and green curtains. To right of the east door, outside, a brass wall tablet states that twenty of Pitt's historical black-columns were incorporated

Photo by Lt.-Col. H. A. Newell.

COUNCIL CHAMBER, FORT ST. GEORGE, SHOWING PITT'S PILLARS.

in the building by desire of Sir Arthur Lawley, Governor of Madras. To north is a long narrow apartment hung with interesting colour prints of Old Madras. This is where the Executive assembles presided over by a full length portrait of Sir Arthur Lawley. Beyond, again, is the Luncheon Room.

THE ARSENAL.

The Arsenal dates from November 9th, 1772, and is one of the various important public works undertaken during the Governorship of Mr. Du Pre (1770-1775). It occupies the site of the old Artillery Park, which was transferred there from its original position to north of the Fort Square. Colonel Ross of the Engineers supervised the construction. The contractor was Mr. John Sullivan, who had come out to Madras in 1765 as a Writer at the age of seventeen. The building cost pagodas 28,000 and comprised two blocks at right angles to one another. Apparently the design of the first storey, which was bomb-proof, presented some difficulty consisting as it did of a series of inverted arches. Colonel Ross was censured for introducing ornamentation on the upper part of the edifice.

The gate opens into Charles and James Street, and is guarded by two brass cannon cast in 1786, a couple of mortars and piles of old ball. Within is a second door beside which a sentry is posted. The courtyard is overlooked by an imposing portico surmounted by two yellow lions in high relief supporting a coat of arms, while the corners of the roof bristle with weapons, armour and gigantic helmets modelled in plaster. The florid style of the decoration is similar to that adorning the hybrid palaces of the last Nawabs of Oudh built at the same period in Lucknow. To south is a three-storied yellow building reserved for the clerical establishment of the Chief Ordnance Officer in charge of Madras Arsenal. Tradition asserts that this was the house inhabited by Colonel Arthur Wellesley, afterwards Duke of Wellington.

THE HOSPITAL.

The earliest hospital was established by Sir Edward Winter, who, in 1664, appropriated Cogan's old house for the accommodation of sick soldiers. Seamen were also admitted. Several years later it was extended. Even so the space was insufficient and public subscriptions provided a larger and better building, in 1679. This was two storeys high and stood near St. Mary's Church. With the arrival of Charnock, and the entire establishment of Bengal, there was a dearth of quarters in the Fort. This led to the Governor purchasing the Hospital from the Vestry for pagodas 838, its original cost. Henceforward it was known as the College. The upper floor was assigned to the Company's Civil Servants, and the lower used for godowns. Unmarried factors and writers lived under the north and south curtains of the Inner Fort.

The Vestry expended the greater part of the money, which they had received for their hospital, in building a new one to the north-west of the Citadel between the Guard's House and carpenter's yard. In 1699 they asked to be relieved of the charge, whereupon the hospital was taken over by the Company, and its doors opened to all necessitous patients without distinction. A surgeon was appointed at an annual salary of £36. For two centuries it continued as a joint military and civil institution. A new and larger building was erected in 1712. Its walls covered part of the site of Agent Greenhill's old residence in Choultry Gate Street, and was in line with the Free Guard House and Mint. The management was vested in the Governor and Council, Ministers and Church-wardens. In 1752 it was decided to remove the Hospital to Peddanaikapetta and to convert the old premises into barracks. Twelve houses, mostly belonging to Portuguese, were appropriated for the new Hospital, near the centre of what is now the Esplanade. The site was opposite to the existing Ordnance Lines. At that time the ground was slightly elevated, hence its name of Hog Hill. Strategical reasons caused Sir Eyre Coote to urge its being levelled, which was accomplished at considerable labour and expense. Again, in 1757, the Hospital was moved to a position near the present General Hospital.

THE MINT.

Permission to establish a Mint in Fort St. George formed one of the clauses of the gold-plated kaul, dated July 22nd, 1639, which Francis Day received from Naik Damela Vintutedra. Seemingly the work of coining began as early as 1640. Down to Ivie's time it was in the hands of Chetties, who contracted for it and made about 4 or 5 per cent profit. In those days the Mint was known as the Darealzarib, from the Persian, Dar-ul-zarab, or house of striking coin. During Ivie's term as Agent, or immediately afterwards, the Mint was taken over by the Company. In a report, dated December 1654, Greenhill states that he employed Englishmen in it. At that period a great variety of coin was current on the Coromandel Coast. Subsidiary coinage struck in the Fort consisted of fanams and cash. The latter was of gold largely intermixed with alloy and was worth three pence. The cash was of copper. In Madras money, eighty cash went to a fanam. The pagoda was of gold estimated at eight shillings and four pence. Silver rupees were not struck until later. Silver dollars, also spoken of as ryalls or pieces of eight, were imported and passed current. By 1656 they had considerably depreciated in value and only equalled five shillings. The Mint was free to all, nevertheless merchants complained greatly of the long delay in converting their bullion into coin. It was a criminal offence to coin money privately. All had to pass through the Mint in Fort St. George.

The Madras pagoda was a flat disc about five-eighths of an inch in diameter impressed with a figure of Vishnu which emitted rays. The reverse was plain. The cash bore a date and the Company's mark, a circle surrounding a cross, in which were the letters 'G.E.C.' The Sultan of Golcondah's pagoda was similar in size and shape to that struck by the merchants. On the reverse were Devanagir characters giving the name of the conquered Vijianagar sovereign. Negotiations with Golcondah failed to secure a firman permitting the coinage of silver rupees. In 1683 the Company procured the desired sanction from King James II of England. After the fall of Golcondah Prince Kam Buksh, son of the Moghul Emperor Aurangzib, authorised the minting of money at Fort St. George. Furthermore he forwarded Governor Yale six imperial chopps, or stamps for gold mohurs, pagodas and rupees. The last were rated at two shillings and two pence halfpenny.

Under Governor Higginson (1692-98) the Mint was rebuilt at the southern end of the block of barracks known as New House, and appears to have coined both gold and silver. Later on, the Gold Mint was established in the Fort Square and the Silver Mint in the north-west angle of White Town, under the bastion which perpetuates its memory. Here a subsequent Mint was erected on an improved plan in 1727. It was double storied. The lower floor provided accommodation for weighing and storing bullion, and also for workshops where the process of coining, smelting and refining was carried on. The Assay Master's quarters were upstairs. He exercised the real control of affairs although the Governor was styled Mint Master and received an honorarium for the same. In 1800 Lord Clive recognised the purely nominal relations existing between the Governor and the Mint and severed the connection. The combined duties of Assay and Mint Master were assigned to the Sub-Treasurer, who was also styled the Paymaster. His offices were in the Fort Square whence he was promptly ordered to remove to the Mint House in April 1800, as the old Gold Mint was about to be demolished.

When Dost Ali Khan, Nawab of the Carnatic (1732-40) closed his Mints at San Thomé and Covelong, he agreed to the transfer of the Poonamallee Mint to one at Chintadripetta. Subsequently the San Thomè Mint was re-opened. At this Governor Benyon (1735-44) prohibited the further coining of Arcot rupees at Chintadripetta. He ordered all required for circulation in Calcutta to be issued by the Fort Mint. In 1741 star pagodas (so called from a star stamped on the reverse) became the standard coin in Southern India, and continued such until early in the nineteenth century. Old Madras pagodas, representing Vishnu and his two wives, were still produced for circulation in the northern settlements. During the course of the eighteenth century the Fort Mint struck star and Madras pagodas, Madras and Arcot gold mohurs, Madras and Arcot rupees, in addition to various lesser coin.

BARRACKS.

The earliest barracks date from 1684. They were erected in Tuscan style by Governor Gifford on the west side of White Town facing the main gate of the Inner Fort. New House was the name given to them and they contained quarters for the Free Guard. Regulations required all to be indoors when the tattoo beat at 9 P.M. To north was the Hospital erected by Yale in 1690. The Mint was to the south, but proved so inconvenient a neighbour that it was transferred to the north-west angle of the ramparts, and its site absorbed by the barracks. These last were rebuilt in 1711 and still further extended. In 1753 they took in the hospital.

What were styled the New Barracks were situated in the South Curtain. In 1770 they were occupied by invalids, and condemned by General Joseph Smith as "so exceedingly close and unhealthy" as to be unsuited for anything but godowns. The barracks, in common with all other houses and streets in the Fort area, were lit by globe lamps burning cocoanut oil.

The block of buildings in Choultry Gate Street, styled King's Barracks, was erected in 1755. A year later the 39th Foot, otherwise the King's Regiment, now the 1st Battalion of the Dorsets, arrived in Madras from Fort St. David, and were the earliest troops to occupy the new quarters. An Army Order, issued in 1782, stipulated that the senior officer, two Field officers, seventeen Captains and twenty-eight subalterns should reside in King's Barracks.

THE GARRISON.

When Day and Cogan arrived at Madras, in February 1640, they were accompanied by the garrison from Armegam, namely twenty-five men, a Lieutenant and a Sergeant. This little force formed the nucleus of the famous Coast Army of later years. Fort St. George was designed to accommodate a garrison of a hundred. Dutch records of 1642 describe it as manned by thirty-five Europeans and an equal number of soldiers raised locally. In 1656 the Court of Directors resolved that their factory of Madraspatam should constantly possess sixty European troops. Despite this the following year found it with thirty-three only. This number was further depleted by a loan of half a dozen men to serve Mir Jumla's artillery. An official report, dated 1673, gives the total strength as twenty-four British Infantry, fourteen artillery, a hundred and sixty-three Portuguese militia, and five hundred and fifty Indian peons.

Streynsham Master attached much importance to military discipline. In 1678 the officers of the garrison petitioned for the grant of commissions, relative rank, and increased pay. The first two requests were granted. The third was referred to London. A table of precedence was drawn up entitling Captains to rank with Senior Merchants, Lieutenants with Merchants, Ensigns with Factors, and Sergeants with Writers. Furthermore it was laid down that the officer of the Guard should dine and sup at the Company's public table in the Citadel. In his dual capacity of Governor and Commander-in-Chief of Fort St. George, Streynsham Master proceeded to confer commissions. Subsequently, when a military Commander-in-Chief of the Army was appointed, the Governor of Madras still exercised supreme military command inside the Fort. This prerogative was voluntarily relinquished by Sir Charles Trevelyan in 1859. Another of Master's decisions affected the posting of notices at the Main Guard. He ruled that standing orders for the Garrison should continue to be displayed there as heretofore. Those concerning the Company's civilians were to be henceforward posted in the Chapel. Courts Martial were instituted.

In July, 1679, the Company had a large stock of unsaleable red cloth on their hands. This they decided to utilise in fitting out the garrison, both British and Portuguese, with uniforms doubled with green calico. The cost was to be borne by the men themselves. English troops received a third of their pay while in India. The remainder was held for them in England, or else was remitted to their families.

The downfall of Golcondah, and consequent fear of Moghul aggression caused the Company to urge the strengthening of the garrison. They desired the Governor to raise a squadron of volunteer cavalry and two infantry companies of militia. The latter were termed train bands. One was composed of the Company's civil servants and English freemen, and the other of Portuguese.

In 1687 the auxiliary guard of two hundred and eighty peons, whose duty it was to patrol the suburbs, were divided into three regular companies, each commanded by an English officer, and further dignified with a red banner.

At the beginning of 1689 Fort St. George only possessed two companies of regulars. The arrival of Charnock, with the entire force from Bengal, greatly enhanced the strength of the Madras garrison. Four companies were formed. These were respectively commanded by Captain James Butt, and Lieutenants Seaton, Sinclare and Troughton. In addition, each possessed an ensign, four sergeants. four corporals and four rounders. Two companies were on duty daily. Half one company guarded the Inner Fort, and the other half were posted at San Thomé Gate, in the outer south wall, James Bulwark, on the east front, the Sea Gate and Charles Point. The second company were detailed to various places in White and Black Towns. Soon Seaton's Company were promoted to be Grenadiers with extra pay. Their exclusive duty was to guard the Citadel.

Yale exerted himself to develop the militia and promote military efficiency. Among the rules which he drew up for the Artillery, one of the principal provisions was that the Gunner, or his Chief Mate must be continuously on duty in the Gun Room. When the tattoo sounded at 9 P.M. gunners' mates were required to instantly repair to their stations and remain at them until beat of drum at dawn. The Company fully supported Yale in all these measures. In a letter to him they say :—" We must forever after keep ourselves a martial nation, in India."

The men messed at the New House, or Free Guard, otherwise the large block of barracks opposite the main entrance to the citadel on the west. Dinner was at 11 A.M. and supper at 6 P.M.

At the time of the French attack in 1746, the Madras garrison was in a weak depleted condition. An old Swede, named Eckman, was in command with the courtesy title of Captain. After the restoration of Fort St. George in 1749, the settlement was not again seriously threatened until Lally's attempt in 1758, by which period the garrison consisted of 1,767 Europeans, and 2,200 sepoys. Their strength was seriously depleted in 1767, when the ravages of Haider Ali's troops, who advanced to the immediate neighbourhood of the Company's Garden House, necessitated continuous reinforcements being sent out to the opposing army under Colonel Joseph Smith. To make good the loss it was found expedient to arm all European civilians, including Portuguese and Armenians. In the subsequent campaigns against Haider Ali and Tipu Sultan, Fort St. George played a memorable part.

Modern weapons of war have completely revolutionised the art of defence with the result that the strongholds regarded as practically impregnable by our grandfathers, are now pronounced obsolete. Fort St. George is no exception to this rule.

GOVERNMENT.

The affairs of Fort St. George were directed by a Council, the members of which were styled merchants. Nothing new or original was attempted in the way of the constitution, which was modelled upon that of the older factory at Bantam. At first the Senior Merchant was known as Agent. In 1653 he was advanced to the dignity of President. The title of Governor was conferred upon him in 1666. Whatever his official designation he was invariably the Senior

Member of Council. The Book-keeper was second, the Warehouse-keeper third, and the Customer, or Collector of Sea Customs, fourth. They met every Monday and Thursday at 8 A.M.. when all matters concerning the Company were laid before them. The Secretary kept a daily record, a copy of which was sent to England once a year. To this the Court of Directors replied in a general letter. Europeans were tried by the Governor and Council in the Fort, before a jury of twelve Europeans. Ordinary justice was administered by the Customer who, as Magistrate of Black Town, sat in the Choultry Court on Tuesdays and Fridays, attended by the Mint Master and Sub-Treasurer. The punishments were of a drastic nature and savoured of the spirit of the times. In the event of a Peon being found asleep, or absent from his post, the Sea Customer condemmed him to be whipped from Point to Point, to receive five lashes at each of the five stipulated places and then dismissed. For murder the culprit was sentenced to death at the common place of execution, and further to suffer the post mortem penalty of hanging in chains from a gibbet overlooking the Poonamallee High Road. The Execution Post, where offenders were shot, stood in front of the main gate of the Fort House, to west. The gibbet was placed near the stable door, probably in the north-west angle of White Town. Other gibbets were on the Island and Poonamallee High Road.

As Commander-in-Chief of the garrison the Governor was responsible for maintaining order in White Town. In Black Town and the neighbouring pettahs, this duty was assigned to a local official styled the Pedda Naik. He controlled the watch, a species of police force, numbering twenty peons. This was soon increased to fifty. The post was hereditary and carried with it certain pains and privileges. Were any one robbed the Pedda Naik was bound to make good the loss by compensating the victim. On the other hand, he was authorised to levy petty taxes upon grain, fuel, oil, fish and betel-nut. Furthermore he was given, rent free, a strip of land for rice fields, in Comerpetta (Weaver's Hamlet) now known as Peddanaikapetta, his title having outlived his office,

In 1675 the Company established definite grades in the Civil Service. Apprentices served seven years. During the first five their annual salary was £5 and was increased to £10 for the last two. They then became Writers for a year pending promotion to Factors at £20. Thereafter they rose to be Merchants on £50. The Governor received £200 a year plus a gratuity of £100. In Pigot's day this was increased to £3,000. At the present time the salary of the Governor of Madras is Rupees 10,000 a month, to which are added Rupees 94,000 annually as household and tour allowance, and Rupees 7,500, or furniture allowance.

The Second in Council was paid £100 per annum, the Third £70 and the Fourth £50. All were provided with free board and lodging. Other members of the establishment were the Chaplain, whose stipend was £100, and the Schoolmaster at £50.

Considerable power was wielded by the Company's Chief Merchant. The first to hold the coveted position was Seshadu Nayak. He was succeeded, in Ivie's time, by the well-known Brahmin, Venkata Verona, head of the Joint Stock Company known as Cassa Verona and Co. He was entrusted with all the Company's investments, and purchased both the goods imported by them, and those intended for export to Europe. At his death, in 1680, the Fort fired a salute of thirty guns.

In his novel "The Surgeon's Daughter," Sir Walter Scott depicts the influence wielded by the Dubash of Fort St. George, who, in his role of interpreter, was frequently the Governor's mouthpiece in dealing with neighbouring powers. Scott introduces this character in the person of Papaiya, who flourished in Madras during the latter half of the eighteenth century. As three of the Author's immediate relatives were in the Company's service at about that epoch it is possible that he obtained his information first hand.

MANNERS AND CUSTOMS.

In all probability the manners and customs characteristic of society at Fort St. George, in the 17th and 18th centuries, reflected those prevalent in England at that period. That they should undergo certain changes, after importation into India, was inevitable, owing to altered conditions, climate, local influences and the isolated position of the settlement, which constituted it more or less of a law unto itself. Much reproach has been uttered concerning the morals of the community, who were accused of unduly frequenting the taverns of Black Town. Men drank hard. Gambling with cards and dice was a popular diversion, as was cock fighting. Brawls, squabbling and duels were common occurrences. So they were in Europe'

Of a truth, the poor follows had little enough diversion of a legitimate kind. They lived together, eat at one common table and attended daily prayers under the suspicious eye of the Governor. On week days they were kept hard at work. There were contracts to be made with local dealers, advances to be doled out to weavers, merchandise to be examined and appraised at the Custom House by the Sea Gate, precious metals, diamonds from Golcondah, pearls from Ceylon and the Persian Gulf, and other gems to be weighed and tested. English goods had to be displayed and a market found for them, always with due regard to the competition of foreign rivals, particularly the Dutch. Book-keeping, invoices and bills of lading claimed much time, so that everyone, from the apprentice at £5 per annum, to the Governor at £200, may be fairly said to have earned his living.

Great excitement was caused in 1678 by the arrival of three maiden ladies.

Streynsham Master (1677-81) introduced much show of state into the administration. A rule already existed forbidding umbrellas to be carried by any but Members of Council, Chiefs of Factories, Commanders of ships from England and the Chaplain. This prohibition affected ladies below the rank of Factor's wife. No foreigner, resident or otherwise, might wear a sword, or weapon of any description, inside the Fort. Even high state officials, who desired to visit the Governor, were required to deposit their arms at the Main Guard.

The chief meal was taken before midday, and was followed by a siesta. The hours were adapted to those of the Custom House, which were from 8 A.M. to 11 A.M. and from 2 P.M. until 4 P.M. A steward, appointed from among the factors, was in charge of the general table at the Fort House, the linen and plate. In Fort St. David this duty was discharged by Robert Clive.

Christmas Day, Easter, St. George's Day, the King's Birthday, Restoration and Guy Fawkes Day were regarded as public holidays. The cannon thundered a salute, and three volleys of small shot were fired. Wine and arrack were served out to the garrison, and punch circulated generously.

On the arrival of a vessel her guns saluted the Fort, which returned the compliment in kind. The Commander proceeded to dine with the

Governor who, not infrequently, made him an offer for the entire cargo before the meal was finished.

Writing of Madras, in 1715, Father Norbert mentions that it was customary for one of the priests attached to the Capuchin Mission, to dine at the Governor's table every Sunday.

HIGH COURT.

Crowned by a number of lesser domes, and one tall central cupola, the great block of red buildings, known collectively as the High Court, is one of the handsomest and most imposing piles in the City. It has practically two faces. One looks eastward across Light House Road, where the low boundary wall displays a small granite tablet inscribed :—"During the bombardment of Madras by the German cruiser 'Emden,' on the night of 22nd September 1914, a shell struck this spot and carried away a portion of the compound wall." On the north side the building fronts China Bazaar Road, Inaugurated in 1861 the High Court of Madras absorbed those earlier institutions, the Faujdar Adaulat, or Chief Criminal Court, and the Sudder Adaulat, or Chief Court of Civil Judicature for the final hearing of appeals. In 1862 letters patent were granted appointing a Chief Justice and five Puisne Judges, with power to administer justice as a Court of Law and Equity, of Oyer and Terminer and General Gaol Delivery, of Ecclesiastical Jurisdiction and of Admiralty. The number of Judges has since been increased to twelve, including the Chief Justice.

At first the High Court was lodged in a more modest edifice to north of its present site. The Judges considered the buildings unsuitable, and the locality too noisy, hence the present pile was commenced in 1889 The interior consists of a labyrinth of vestibules, corridors, stairways and courts, intricate and bewildering as the mazes of the law itself. On the first floor four straight galleries merge in a square central hall dominated by a dim figure, turban crowned and majestic. Nearer approach reveals a fine white marble statue of Sir T. Muthusami Iyer, Judge of the High Court from 1878 to 1895. This monument to his memory was erected by public subscription.

THE LIGHT HOUSE.

The tall tower of the High Court combines use with ornament, being also the Light House. Its dome is the work of distinguished masons, Lord Lansdowne, Lord Wenlock and Sir Arthur Collins each having laid a stone of it. Visitors are admitted from 8 to 11 A.M. and again from 1 to 5 P.M. The climb is somewhat strenuous. Winding stairs lead up a narrow corner turret to a vast roof. A second turret, to north-east, contains more corkscrew steps. When fifty have been mounted the stranger is ushered into a big room. Here he is required to sign his name in a book and pay a fee of two annas. Thereafter a dizzy iron stair twists round and up a giddy height to the light house, The encircling balcony commands a wide-flung panorama of city, sea and plain stretching to the horizon, excepting where interrupted by the shadowy outline of the Eastern Ghats. Immediately below, to east, the eye is caught by four large red buildings singularly bare and curiously alike. These are the property of the Port Trust. Between them and the sea rise the circular grey forms of gigantic iron oil tanks. They constitute admirable targets. As such they were fired at in September 1914 by the enemy cruiser "Emden." The flat expanse, which separates the tanks from the most southerly of the square red houses, is utilised as an engineering yard by the Asiatic Petroleum Company. Here those kerosene tins are manufactured which form so familiar a feature in the India of to-day. The works date from 1912.

OLD LIGHT HOUSE.

Few would imagine that the graceful fluted column to south-east of the High Court had once been a lighthouse. Beautifully fitted stone blocks of Pallavaram gneiss lend the pillar an appearance of solidity and strength, and allow no hint to transpire of the brick framework. The design is that of a Greek Doric column 125 feet in height, and originated with Captain J. E. Smith of the Madras Engineers, who began to excavate the foundations on 17th July 1838. These were sunk ten feet below the ground to receive a forty feet square base of laterite, from which the brickwork foundation rose in a compact masonry block. Lord Elphinstone and a distinguished gathering witnessed the laying of the first stone on September 19th of the same year. The building was completed in December 1843 and the lamp lit on New Year's Day, 1844. It is said to have been visible fifteen miles out at sea.

Now the top of the column has a dismantled look suggestive of a pedestal that has lost its statue, hence the proposal to use it as a flagstaff. In view of its close proximity to the Law Courts a figure of Justice would seem by far the most appropriate substitute. Robbed of its light by its legal neighbour, and overshadowed,it might at least shine with a reflected glory. By all means let it have justice.

LAW COLLEGE.

Near neighbour to the High Court, on the west, is yet another imposing block of red buildings designed by Mr. Irwin, the Government Architect. It, too, is in the approved style of Indo-Saracenic architecture characteristic of the latter half of the 19th century. This edifice is the Law College and, with the playground behind, occupies the site of the old English burial ground on the confines of the original Black Town. During the French siege of 1758-59 the towering gravestones afforded valuable cover to Lally's army. This led to their being demolished, and the inscribed portions transferred to St. Mary's Church in the Fort, where they pave the outer enclosure to north-east. A couple of tombs still retain their positions in the ancient cemetery. The most conspicuous stands in the north-west corner of the tennis courts. It is a tall pointed building of quaint design tunneled by a central passage, on the northern wall of which is an elaborately carved panel to David, the only son of Governor Elihu Yale. The little lad died on Jannary 25th, 1687. Exactly opposite is a second mural tablet to Joseph Hynmers, whose widow Yale married, It bears the date May 28th, 1680.

Two tennis courts intervene between this grave and a large square stone vault to east shaded by a spreading rain tree. Here sleep four members of the Powney family, and Captain George Heron, the first to be interred here in 1725. He was father-in-law to Captain John Powney, also buried underneath. The Powney family were well known in Madras throughout the 18th century. They were chiefly sailors. The earliest of the name came to Fort St. George in 1703. Captain Heron was marine surveyor and master mariner. When seventy-five years of age he was British Resident at Pegu, where his name figures in 1721 in connection with a maritime dispute. The very site of the old burial ground had been forgotten until excavations for the foundations of the Law College brought to light a number of skeletons.

THE CHRISTIAN COLLEGE.

To north of the High Court a handsome bronze statue looks across China Bazaar Road to a block of buildings comprising the Christian

College, church and hostels appertaining thereto. The important educational effort, which these represent, originated with the Rev. John Anderson, a Free Church Missionary, who founded a school and church on the site in 1837. The bronze monument commemorates a well-loved labourer in the same field, namely William Miller, L.L.D., C.I.E., for many years Principal of the College. His statue was erected by public subscription and unveiled by Lord Ampthill in 1901.

CHINA BAZAAR ROAD,

This thoroughfare derives its name from a series of bazaars of which chinaware originally formed the chief commodity. Now practically any article may be procured in one or other of the many shops. The area is a popular one with bargain hunters. Historically the road is deeply interesting. Not only did it constitute the northern boundary of old Black Town; it is believed to have been the site of the northern rampart erected by Ivie (1644-48). Late in 1758 it was converted into a battlefield, where a sharp fight developed when Colonel Draper sought to repel a French attempt to carry Fort St. George from that side. It was on the 14th of December. Already at daybreak the French had crossed the Triplicane River, advanced unopposed through Vepery and established themselves in Black Town. They then proceeded to hoist the French flag above the Armenian Church.

A sally being determined upon, Colonel Draper issued from the west gate of the Fort at 8-30 A.M., followed by a force six hundred strong. Meanwhile the French had placed the Lorraine and Indian Regiments in China Bazaar. Here Draper attacked them. The fight continued until the English Commander found his retreat threatened by a fresh body of the enemy, who advanced from the Armenian Church. At this he moved eastward along China Bazaar to join a small detachment under Major Brereton. The junction effected, it was decided to regain the Fort. This was accomplished but with the loss of over a third of the original force. British casualties amounted to nine officers and more than two hundred men. The enemy's punishment was heavier still, being thirty officers and two hundred and twenty men. In addition, Brigadier-General Comte d'Estaing had been made prisoner.

ARMENIAN STREET.

At the northern side of China Bazaar, to west of the Christian College, lies Armenian Street, so called from the old Armenian cemetery once situated on the ground now covered by the Armenian Church near the south-west corner of the road. In the early days of Fort St. George special privileges were offered to Armenian settlers. Sir John Child induced the Company, in 1688, to grant members of that nation the same rights as those enjoyed by English freemen. Nor was this all. Wherever an Armenian community numbered forty, the Company undertook to build a church for them, and allow the priest £50 annually for the first seven years. By these means quite a large Armenian population was attracted to Madras. Apparently they limited themselves to trading, and took no interest in public affairs for, in 1693, it was complained that they declined to serve on the Corporation.

The entrance to the Church is marked by a high gateway surmounted by a cross and the date 1712. Inside is an old-world courtyard shaded with palms and other trees, and paved with red brick and large gravestones. The latter are inscribed with Armenian characters, and a variety of quaint and curious devices, amid which scales of justice, skulls and crossbones figure frequently. In a line with the gate stands the belfry, a detached yellow tower crowned by a cupola and a slender cross. A little distance to north is the Church, likewise yellow and white, surrounded by a deep many-pillared verandah, with gravestones for floor. With his long black beard, sweeping robes of the same sable hue, and high head dress the priest seems strangely in keeping with the spirit of the place.

During the second half of the 18th century the Government of Fort St. George appropriated the Armenian cemetery, with its small Church, and the neighbouring Capuchin burial ground to north for the erection of temporary hospitals. Both sites were restored in 1772, when preparations were made for erecting the existing sanctuaries.

ROMAN CATHOLIC CATHEDRAL.

Also situated on the west side of Armenian Street the Cathedral is a somewhat bare building of little architectural interest. The gate bears the date 1642, and probably refers to a grant of the site, in that year, as a graveyard, to the Capuchin mission. The large grey house to the north was occupied by Lally, Commander-in-Chief of the French Army, which besieged Madras in 1758-59.

NORTH BEACH ROAD.

Many of the most notable buildings in Madras stretch along the western side of North Beach Road to the harbour, beginning at Parry's corner, so called from the premises of the well-known mercantile firm now occupying the site. This point played an important part during the second siege of Madras by the French. Here the famous Regiment de Lally were quartered. Near by, on the beach, to east of the Doric column known as the Old Light House, was Lally's battery of fifteen heavy guns, whence a zigzag was pushed with skill and daring close up to the north-east wall of Fort St. George. The firm of Parry and Company is the oldest British Association of the kind in the city. Founded by Thomas Parry, of Leighton Hall, Welshpool, it dates from the eighteenth century. Its originator had an eventful career. Tradition avers that he came out to India as super-cargo. At first he appears to have been employed in the Accountant's Office, whence he was transferred to be Secretary to Governor Medows (1792-94). As was customary among the Company's civil servants he indulged in private trading, sometimes on his own account, but, more frequently, in partnership with others, preferably his nephew, David Pugh, and Mr. Charles Breithaupt, also a family connection. With himself these constituted the firm when Parry retired in 1814 to assume charge of the Treasury in the Fort. He rejoined the firm in 1818, but appears to have fallen into disfavour with the Government through befriending certain Indian princes, whose interests were threatened by the rapid political changes of the times. This led to his banishment. Proceeding to Ceylon he remained there as a guest of the Governor until altered conditions favoured his return to Madras. Shortly afterwards he and a young nephew of his fell victims to cholera, when travelling from Porto Novo to Cuddalore. Thomas Parry lies buried at the latter place, in Christ Church, Old Town. St. George's Cathedral, Madras, also contains a tablet to his memory.

Next to Parry and Company come the offices of the Deputy Commissioner of Police, Northern Range, The National Bank of India and the offices of the "Madras Mail," the city's popular evening paper founded in December 1868. The Mercantile Bank and City Police Court follow in rapid succession. The General Post Office covers a wide frontal. Its next-door neighbour is the Registrar General's Office; then comes the grey building of Best and Company and a vacant site reserved for the Mercantile Bank. Beyond, again, is the Indian Bank. The Offices of Government Stationery are included in the spreading yellow block once the High Court, now utilised as the Collector's Office, Presidency Port Office, etc. Immediately in front stands an octagonal stone pavilion, the domed roof supported by clusters of pillars. This is known as the Cenotaph and was erected in honour of Lord Cornwallis after his successful campaign against Tipu Sultan in 1792, the result of which led to immense territorial acquisitions by the Company. The ornamental iron screen work surrounding the upper part of the memorial was cast from guns captured by Cornwallis at Seringpatam. Originally the Cenotaph stood midway between Madras and St. Thomas Mount, whence it was removed to its present position.

On the opposite side of the street stand the Port Health Office and Harbour House. The offices of Government Consignments and Customs occupy the corner of the road, whence a side street runs west to the Supply Depot.

THE HARBOUR.

The term benighted, occasionally applied to Madras by those ignorant, or forgetful of the momentous part which the city has played in shaping the destinies of British India, undoubtedly originated in the drawback under which it long laboured of being a port town without a harbour. This disadvantage has now been entirely overcome, although during the cyclone season (April-June and October-November) ships have occasionally to leave the harbour, and proceed to sea for a few hours. The reason for this precautionary measure is that, otherwise, the wind pressure might cause them to break their own lines. It is not on account of waves as, no matter what weather conditions prevail, steamers lie in still water.

The harbour is an artificial one formed by two arms projecting from the flat sandy coast. The entrance is 400 feet wide, with a depth of 39 feet at high water and 34 feet at low. The enclosed area is about three-quarters of a mile square and approximates 200 acres, with a general depth of 30 feet at low water. Ten sets of moorings are provided for vessels of from 20 to 30 feet draught, although twelve can be accommodated if necessary. There are no docks at present. The new West Quay has a length of 3,000 feet and berths four steamers with 26, 28, and 30 feet at low water. In addition, there are four other quays, one drawing 28 feet and three 25 feet. Each can accommodate one vessel at a time at low tide. Lighters, however, still do the bulk of landing and shipping. Of these, fifty are over 40 tons and 180 under. About 4,000 tons of cargo can lie afloat at one time, two-thirds of it being in modern well found lighters. Three or four tugs are available for towing purposes.

Loading and unloading by means of lighters is done along a frontage some three-quarters of a mile in extent. This space comprises ferro-concrete wharves, and a portion of the West Quay equipped with hand, steam and hydraulic cranes of from one to thirty-eight tons capacity. Adjacent to the wharves are eight acres of temporary shedding and five acres of warehouses for leasing to exporters. A slipway is provided for the repair of craft under 400 tons. Two large quayed ponds for bar iron and timber are fitted with cranes, railways and other special facilities for the trades concerned. Colliers discharge about 1,200 tons per day, into railway wagons, at each of the three quays. Large passenger vessels habitually use two of the quays having direct railway connection. Oil, from bulk oil steamers, is pumped ashore at four places, likewise petrol at a special berth. Conveniences for troop trains, horses and cattle are provided.

Ships get their water from boats selling water from the city municipal supply. It is possible for vessels to enter or leave the harbour at any hour. Usually, however, they are only allowed to do so during daylight.

The affairs of the harbour are directed by the Madras Port Trust Board, of which Sir Francis Spring, K.C.I.E., M.INST.C.E., was for so long the well-known Chairman and Chief Engineer. He has been succeeded by Lt.-Col. H. H. G. Mitchell, M.I.C.E. Mr. W. W. Robinson is the Traffic Manager. Springhaven Road perpetuates Sir Francis Spring's notable work in constructing the harbour, the immense stone blocks of which were quarried at Pallavaram, 11 mile south of Madras.

The project of providing the city with a harbour reached maturity during the Governorship of the late Lord Hobart who, in 1873, approved a plan for overcoming the difficulties of the surf. Two years afterwards the scheme was sanctioned. When the King-Emperor Edward VII visited Madras in 1875, as Prince of Wales, he laid the Memorial Stone, which now stands immediately to south-west of the handsome granite gateway marking the entrance to the harbour.

KASIMODE.

Flat and sandy, the coast stretches northward to Kasimode (Royapuram Division), a quarter much discussed owing to the doubtful origin of its name. Popular tradition asserts that it perpetuates the visit of an old-time King of Kashi (Benares) who travelled southwards from his holy city on the left bank of the Ganges, to attend the annual Natalam festival at Tiruvotiyur, a mile and a half to north of Kasimode, where the principal temple is dedicated to Nataraja, the dancing form of Siva. Unfortunately the sovereign arrived too late for the ceremony. Not to be diverted from his pious purpose he waited until the following year. In support of this the Kasi Kolam, or Benares Tank, is pointed out at Tiruvotiyur, and the visitor is told that it was dug by the king, who subsequently bathed therein.

Another tradition assigns the origin of the name to Kashipur, a saint, who dwelt on a mode, or elevated spot in the neighbourhood. Yet a third version ascribes it to Kasim, a noted Muhammadan gymnast, who made his home there.

FIRST DAY.........*Afternoon.*

Drive via Government House Road and the Marina to Mylapore. Visit the Aquarium and San Thomé Cathedral. Proceed by Elphinstone Bridge to Adyar and Elliot's Beach.

GOVERNMENT HOUSE.

Iron railings and a deer park surround the stately white building known as Government House, a title conferred upon it in 1753, in which year it was bought for pagodas 3,500 from the widow of Luis Madera, or Madeiros, a wealthy free merchant, who figures in the records of 1711 as Commander of the good ship "Messiah." Prior to its acquisition by Government the property was raided by the

French in 1746, shortly after they had wrecked the Company's Garden House at Peddanaikapetta. The latter stood on the site now occupied by the General Hospital. When Madras was again declared the seat of Government in 1752, it was decided to purchase Mrs. Madeiros' residence, with its long garden and ornamental pond, for Governor Saunders, in place of the ruined Garden House. Since then both park and house have been considerably enlarged.

The main gate opens into Mount Road. On entering, attention is first attracted by a classical white building approached by a long flight of steps. This is the Banqueting Hall erected by Edward, Lord Clive, in 1802, to commemorate the fall of Seringapatam. The Parthenon, at Athens, was the model selected for the upper storey. In addition to the great central chamber, the edifice contains a number of basement rooms. The walls of the hall are hung with fine oil paintings portraying various famous men of Madras who have figured prominently in British history. Several of the portraits originally adorned the interior of the Exchange now the Officers' Mess in Fort St. George.

To north of Government House flows the Cooum River. Wallajah Road bounds it to south, taking its name from that well-known Nawab of the Carnatic, Muhammad Ali (1749-75) popularly styled Wallajah. His successor, Umdat-ul-Amara, was the first Indian to become a Freemason, having been initiated at Trichinopoly, in 1775, by Dr. Terence Gahagan.

THE MARINA.

This fine macadamised road starts from the Iron Bridge across the mouth of the Cooum, whence it stretches southward along the sea front to the old Portuguese town of San Thomé in Mylapore. It constitutes the favourite afternoon resort of Madras, hence the variety of wheeled traffic encountered, ranging from the motor-cars of Government House, the Maharajas, and the Prince of Arcot down to the humble bandy, still more modest rickshaw, and even the homely bullock cart. The Band of the Madras Guards, I.D.F. plays on Monday afternoons. and also on moonlight nights, The city owes the Marina to Sir M. E. Grant Duff, who was appointed Governor in 1881. Prior to that the popular rendezvous was on Band Practice Road to north of the Cooum, near the walls of Fort

St. George. It bore the significant nickname of Cupid's Bow. On its western side a tan riding course separates the Marina from the stately official buildings which look across it towards the sea. The thoroughfare only lacks an avenue of trees to make it one of the finest of its kind in the world.

MARINE VILLA.

This is the first building on the Marina to north. It stands near the bar of the Cooum, where some fifty people were drowned in 1792 by the capsizing of the ferry boat. Those were the days before the bridge. At that time Marine Villa was styled the Nawab's Octagon, as it was included within the bounds of Chepauk Palace.

SENATE HOUSE.

Architecturally the handsome red Senate House conforms to the ideal, which inspired the majority of public edifices of the same date in India. Commenced in 1874, it was finished five years later at a cost of Rupees 2,89,729. It serves a variety of uses, concerts and an art exhibition among the number. The most important annual ceremony held in its great Hall is the conferring of degrees upon the Alumni of Madras. Lectures are delivered upstairs at the southern end of the building, notably those under the auspices of the Literary Society. The windows command delightful panoramic views of azure sea, sunlit sands and verdant palm topes.

To west of the encircling grounds stands a square masonry block obviously intended as pedestal for a statue. The engraved tablet states :—" This foundation stone was laid by His Excellency the Rt. Hon'ble Charles, Baron Hardinge of Penshurst, Viceroy and Governor-General of India, on November 25th, 1913."

On the southern side is a beautiful white marble statue of the Queen-Empress Victoria donated by Raja Goday Naraen Gajapatee Rao, as a Jubilee memorial. The unveiling ceremony was performed by Lord Connemara on June 20th, 1887. To east, looking on to the Marina, is a life-sized figure of V. Krishnaswami Iyer, C.S.I., Member of the Madras Executive Coucil, born 1863, died 1911. The monument was erected by public subscription.

CHEPAUK PALACE.

Now commonly referred to as Chepauk Palace, this elaborate and picturesque pile was built by Muhammad Ali, eighth Nawab of the Carnatic (1749-95). The design sanctioned by the Nawab emanated from a British officer of Engineers, probably Benfield. It included two blocks arranged in the form of a capital " L," the angle being at the south-west corner. The south wing was double storied and was known as the Khalsa Mahal, or Treasury. The other consisted of a single floor and was styled Humayan Mahal, in honour, possibly, of the Moghul Emperor of that name. It contained the Dewan Khana, a splendid audience chamber described by Lord Valentia, in 1804, as " extremely handsome, of large dimensions and divided by pillars." The property originally belonged to Mahfuz Khan, a brother of the Nawab. The latter acquired it in 1767. Three years afterwards he obtained an additional grant of land from the Governor of Fort St. George, whereupon he enclosed the entire site of 117 acres with a boundary wall, extending 1,130 yards southward from the bar of the Cooum, and 500 yards along the bank of that river. A few years earlier Muhammad Ali had applied for permission to erect a palace for himself inside Fort St. George. This had been granted by Governor Pitt, who allotted a site for the purpose, where the foundation stone was laid with much pomp and ceremony, acccompanied by the usual firing of guns. The Council, however, disapproved the scheme which was ultimately abandoned. Its memory survives in Palace Street, still the chief thoroughfare of the new part of the Fort lying west of Charles and Choultry Gate Streets.

The thirteenth and last Nawab of the Carnatic, Ghulam Muhammad Ghaus Khan, was childless. Upon his death in 1855 the British Government took over the palace. Additions, including the central tower, were made and it was converted into public offices, notably the Board of Revenue and P. W. D., which adjoin the Engineering College.

LADY WENLOCK'S PAVILION,

The Presidency College and its extensive playgrounds divide this last from Lady Wenlock's Pavilion, a small building characterised by a long verandah and two red-tiled roofs, one at either extremity. The Pavilion stands in what is called a park. The enclosure is surrounded by a wall and contains a fountain.

Photo by Wiele & Klein.

THE AQUARIUM.

This is situated on the Beach to east of the Marina, exactly opposite the Presidency College. It contains a most interesting and representative collection of fish, and aquatic marvels common to Madras waters. Merely a nominal fee is charged for admittance to the building, which has passed from the management of the Superintendent of the Central Museum, to that of the Board of Fisheries. Considerable developments are foreshadowed.

THE ICE HOUSE,

Next follows an open stretch dotted with samadhs, the Hindu substitutes for tombstones. These mark the sites of old funeral pyres. Beyond rises a curious white building, three stories high, the roof surmounted by a slender pineapple ornament. Known as the Ice House it was erected about 1842 for the storage of natural ice brought by sea. Now it is used as a Home for Brahmin widows. Close under its southern wall is the fishing village of Nadu Kuppam, behind which stretch various buildings collectively entitled Glass Warehouse.

SHAH AULAIYA'S TOMB.

Such is the popular appellation of the glistening white dome that rises above the encircling green of a palm tope to south-west. It is a noted place of Muhammadan pilgrimage, and is largely patronised on Thursdays. The great Sandal festival, in honour of the Saint's death, is held annually on April 4th. He was a native of Bijapur, and is reputed to have come to Madras in 1757, and to have died in 1772, at a great age on the spot now hallowed by his ashes. His correct style was Muhammad Abdul Huk Khadiri Sufi-ul-Bijapuri, for which the vulgar substituted the shorter and more convenient title of Shaikh-ul-Aulaiya. He belonged to the Sunni sect. His shrine was built, and liberally patronised by Wallajah, the celebrated Nawab of the Carnatic, who resided in the neighbouring palace facing the Marina. The Nawab's descendant, the Prince of Arcot, is also a worshipper at the shrine. So widespread was the saint's fame for sanctity, his gift of prophecy, and the miraculous cures he wrought, that a tradition asserts that those powerful rulers, Haider Ali and Tipu Sultan, were in the habit of coming to pray at his shrine disguised as fakirs. That the sanctuary was a celebrated one is proved by the fact of its figuring in Sir Walter Scott's only Indian novel. Now its glories have somewhat faded, nevertheless it is a romantic spot set amid crumbling Mosques, gravestones and palms. A tank of green water adds yet a further characteristic and picturesque feature. The Durgah lies on the east side of Barber's Bridge Road and is easily found. Under the dome, to east of the saint's tomb, a blank space is pointed out as the spot where the body of Nawab Wallajah lay prior to its transfer to Trichinopoly.

CAPPER HOUSE.

Returning to the Marina, two square white buildings catch the eye. Both are educational institutes for the training of girl students. Between them is a gap marked by a masonry pillar and inscribed grey marble tablet. This is the site of a similar college, the foundation stone of which was laid by Lord Pentland prior to his departure from Madras at the end of March 1919. The next building is Capper House, in turn a Hotel and now a school for girls. Originally it was the residence of Colonel F. Capper. who entered the Army in 1778 and was lost at sea. Beyond, again, are Sir Subramania Iyer's residence, the office of the Inspector-General of Police, once a Masonic lodge, and a stretch of open ground. In front are a few scattered samadhs, and at the back, a Hindu burning ghat. Noachi Kuppam is the large fishing village on the seashore at the southern extremity of the Marina. Beyond, again, are palm trees and the yellow spire of San Thomé Cathedral.

MYLAPORE.

Although the origin of Mylapore, the Peacock City, has become obscured by time, there seems no reason for doubting the age-long tradition that it was once a place of considerable importance, the capital of an early Hindu dynasty. This report is confirmed by its identification as the Mallarpha mentioned by Ptolemy. It was to the Court of one of these forgotten kings (Mahadevan according to the Chronicles of the Catholic Church) that St. Thomas, the Doubting Apostle, came in the first century of our era. After his death a little colony of Armenian Christians established themselves near his tomb, and so kept alive the story of his martyrdom, and the miracles and circumstances connected therewith. From them the Portuguese learnt the tradition when, in 1503, di Albuquerque sailed up the east coast and obtained permission from the Maharaja of Vijianagar, described as "The Lord of the Soil," to found a factory at Mylapore, then a celebrated centre of the cotton weaving industry. Soon churches, monasteries and private residences sprang up around the ancient edifice on the seashore, where the body of the Apostle was believed to have been laid to rest.* Fortifications followed. The encircling wall was 15 feet high and massive in proportion. Block-houses stretched along the sea front, the line of which is still marked by masonry remains and can be clearly traced. The Sea Gate stood on the site now marked by what is known as the old Dutch flagstaff, a wooden pole affixed to a small brick platform. This entrance was so low that a horse could only enter with difficulty. The main gate was to west, which was regarded as the front of the town and so distinguished by a lofty and imposing portal. The enclosed area was twice that of the later English settlement at Fort St. George, Madras. San Thomé di Meliapor was the official style of the Portuguese city.

In 1558 fictitious tales of the wealth stored at San Thomé induced the Vijianagar sovereign to invest the place with a large army. The Portuguese Governor, Constantine de Braganza, would have resisted, but the inhabitants insisted upon surrendering. Accordingly he withdrew to Goa. No sooner had the King of Vijianagar encamped beneath the walls than the citizens sent him a gift of 4,000 ducats. At this he ordered every man, woman and child to assemble before him with all their worldly possessions. A valuation was made and the whole assessed at 80,000 ducats. Finding that he had been deceived, the monarch condemned the treacherous informer to be torn limb from limb by elephants. For their part the people of San Thomé were dismissed to their homes. Their belongings were restored to them with such scrupulous honesty that only a silver spoon was reported missing.

San Thomé rose to its greatest eminence between 1567 and 1582. During this period it was visited by Caesar Frederike, who sailed from Venice in 1563. He says: "The Portuguese have built themselves a city in the country of the King of Vijianagar which city, although not very large, is in my judgment the fairest in that part of the Indies."

The seventeenth century found San Thomé a prey to internal feuds and foreign aggression. Captain Pedro de Rezende was detailed to draw up plans and descriptions of all Portuguese forts in India. These are bound together in a work dated 1646, from which the following is an extract:—"The City of St. Thomé de Meliapor is surrounded by a wall pursuing the line of houses. Its doors, along the shore are almost washed by the waves. Although in ancient times the town, together with the house of the glorious St. Thomas, where he dwelt near a shrine named after the sun, was founded half a league inland, the sea has constantly advanced, as the Saint prophesied, until it is within a hundred paces of the said shrine. It was on account of this house and shrine that the wall was built round the city at this spot. It is 5 yards high, including the parapets which are 10 spans thick at the top. On the sea face are three bulwarks. On the north is the bastion of St. Dominic, with a breastwork in the middle protected by artillery. To south is the bulwark of St. Paul. Before San Dominic bastion is one of the four gates of the city, with a watch tower in front, where guns can be mounted. There are in all twelve bastions. The city artillery comprises thirty iron guns and one of brass, in addition to a swivel gun of forty iron hoops, and four wall pieces. The resident Portuguese amount to a hundred and twenty. The two hundred Native Christians are also capable of bearing arms, as are the servants of the Portuguese. The garrison consist of five hundred musketeers and the Captain of the City, who is usually a nobleman. Great trust is reposed in him. There is no harbour. Ships sent from Goa rarely return without loss and damage.

Many faithful Christians, including six hundred fishermen, live outside the fortifications. His Majesty does not receive as much as a real from Meliapore, as everything belongs to the Lord of the Soil. There are no salaried officials excepting the Bishop, whose stipend of two thousand crosses (approximately Rupees 5,250) is paid from Goa, and the Captain of the City, who is given a like sum. The latter receives half the revenue of the Sea Gate from the Lord of the Soil. At present, on account of the Dutch, this brings in less than a gold Pagoda daily. The city has a circuit of 2,000 paces, and is situated on a spot as flat as the palm of the hand, with a lagoon to southward."

According to Rezende's plan of San Thomé the area within the ramparts was long and narrow. Each of the four sides was pierced by a central gate. The main entrance was in Rosary Church Road, San Thomè owed its downfall to the Dutch. Not only was it the first of the Portuguese possessions in India which they attacked, they established a blockade and captured all vessels bound for the town. Abandoned by Goa, harassed by the Dutch, and besieged by the Muhammadan army of Golcondah, it finally yielded in May, 1662. The Portuguese were ejected and the place strongly garrisoned by two thousand of the Sultan's troops. Manucci gives a vivid accoant of the state of affairs under Moslem control. Writing in 1699 he says :—"San Thomé was taken from the Portuguese by the Kutb Shahi King in 1662, and never restored in sovereignty. They only returned there on suffrance about 1686 . . . . To set forth the matter properly, and the present condition of the town, it is of very great extent. The Muhammadans occupy the most important, and by far the larger part of it. The Portuguese but a narrow space. It is quite true that the Portuguese houses are built right in the centre of the town. All the same they are no longer its masters. On the contrary it may be said they are besieged within it on all sides. The Portuguese exercise no authority. Their principal, in fact their only privilege, is to fly their standard on festivals and on Sundays."

Commanded by General de la Haye a French force stormed the town in 1672. A landing party effected an entrance through the main gate to west, which the conquerors renamed Porte Royale. The French were not left long in undisturbed possession. On July 30th, 1672, the Golcondah forces surrounded San Thomé until March 10th of the following year, when they withdrew, only to return with the Dutch on June 30th. The latter attacked by sea. Their fleet was a strong one, numbering twenty sail, and fifteen men of war armed with seventy-two brass guns apiece. The French garrison held out gallantly until August 24th, 1674, when utter exhaustion of supplies compelled them to surrender. Terms were made with the Dutch to whom General de la Haye delivered the city greatly to the annoyance of Golcondah. The Dutch, however, promptly handed it over to the Sultan.

The loss of San Thomé led Francis Martin to found the famous settlement of Pondicherry upon a site granted to him by Sher Khan Lodi, a representative of the Sultan of Bijiapur in whose territory the land lay. Meanwhile Langhorne, at that time Governor of Madras, urged upon the Sultan of Golcondah to raze San Thomé to the ground. The Dutch seconded him in this proposal. Orders were accordingly issued for the fortifications and principal edifices to be demolished. Gunpowder was used, nevertheless the work took three months. The stones were removed to Madras and speedily utilised for building. Thanks to the intercession of the Moghul Governor of San Thomé the churches were spared.

At various times the Portuguese sought to regain possession. It is reported that the Armenians also strove to become masters of San Thomé. In 1749 it passed to the English.

After its stormy history the ancient town is now quiet enough, its silence charged with many memories. It is traversed by two main streets, the San Thomé High Road, a continuation of the Marina, and Rosary Church Road. The latter starts from the Old Dutch Flagstaff, once the Sea Gate, and runs inland to the celebrated Luz Church.

SAN THOME CATHEDRAL.

It was the first century A. D. The city of Meliaporum, with its palms, its temples and its glistening white palace, lay basking in the hot yellow sunshine. Suddenly a mysterious rumour spread from the kuppams to the bazaar, and thence to the Court and the King himself. Some fishermen, it said, had found the immense trunk of an unknown tree on the seashore. Instantly all repaired to the sands to witness the marvel. There it lay with the blue waves breaking over it in cascades of white surf. The wise pronounced it kalamander wood from the distant island of Ceylon. Now the King, whose name was Mahadevan, commanded coolies to haul the log to his Palace, where skilled carvers would convert it into pillars for his Darbar Hall. Curiously enough strain as they might the coolies could not move the log. Elephants were brought, and then the entire army, but all laboured in vain. The King and his subjects were amazed. Priests were summoned, and propitiatory rites performed without result. When this unsatisfactory state of affairs had continued for some time an aged stranger stepped forward from among the crowd. Addressing the sovereign he asked whether, in the event of his moving the log, he might have it to build a house with? The King was amused by the request, and well he might be, for the stranger was an old man and frail. Laughingly the King acquiesced. At this the stranger unknotted his girdle, tied it about the tree and told a coolie to drag it along. This the coolie accomplished with the greatest of ease. Amazed at the miracle King Mahadevan not only gave the log to the stranger, but also a piece of land, upon which the old man, who was none other than the Holy Apostle Thomas, erected a small Church on the site now covered by the large Portuguese Cathedral of San Thomé. After his martyrdom, on December 21st, A.D. 68, pious hands carried the body of the Saint, and laid it to rest under the floor of the Church that he had built with the miraculous log. Here it lay until, in the 4th century, pilgrims transported it to Edessa. A colony of Armenian Christians kept alive the pious traditions of the place. When the Portuguese arrived, early in the 16th century, they found a small sanctuary on the spot. This they proceeded to enlarge. An inscription, on the north wall of the existing Cathedral, states that the first mass, after the arrival of the Portuguese in India, was celebrated on the tomb of the Saint by the Revd. Antonio Gill, on Corpus Christi Day, 1521. On the opposite wall to north, a second mural tablet gives the names of the Bishops of San Thomé, beginning with Fr. Sebastiano de San Pedro, 1606-14.

The paved floor is closely covered with old gravestones dating from the 16th century. Near the centre of the nave steps lead down to a small narrow tomb, wherein the body of the Apostle is believed to havo reposed for the first four centuries of our era. Here a verger provides a long wooden ladle, by means of which it is possible to scrape up sand from the sepulchre, which was reopened on April 29th, 1729. The sand is credited with healing virtue. Near by, on the north wall of the Cathedral, a brass tablet is inscribed:—"Hic spectabili referente vetere traditione corpus est humatum B. Thomae Apostoli qui, cum diceretur Didymus et unus esset de duodecimi, Lance transfixus ni vicinia, vitam pro fide effudit. Magistri A.D. 68, in quorimi fidem, Henricus Primus, instauratae. (A. D. 1886) diceceseos Episcopus Meliaporensis, Cum Ecclesiam velustam hic existentem ampliandam et ab immis fundamentis di novo erigendam curasset opere feliciter complete taballam hanc conficiendam mandavit, et ipse hic locavit A. D. 1896."

A similar brass plate, on the south wall, says:—"Altari, quod super celebre Apostoli Thomae sepulcrum hic pio affectu extruxit marmoreum perenne monumentum tertii saecularis ab hac sede erecta jubiliaci esse voluit Dmis Theotonius Episcopus Meliaporensis Die 9 Januaria A. D. 1906." The present Cathedral replaces an older and smaller one demolished in 1894. The earlier edifice did not include the Saint's tomb which stood under a little dome. After the French occupied San Thomé, in 1672, General de la Haye proceeded in state to the Cathedral, where a mass was celebrated. The French found that the Muhammadans had taken scrupulous care of all the Portuguese Churches, even going so far as to keep the holy vessels cleaned. Old writers speak much of the veneration shown to the relics of the Apostle. These can be seen on application to the priest in charge, and include a fragment of the spear which is believed to have killed Saint Thomas.

An interesting momento of Portuguese rule survives in a sundial set up in the south-east corner of the Cathedral compound. To north-east is a picturesque grotto of Our Lady of Lourdes. Above the entrance appear the royal arms of Portugal surmounted by a crown. They are engraved on a stone slab originally let into the outer wall of the old Cathedral over the southern door.

The Priory is at the eastern end of the compound, in a line with the Bishop's Palace, a pleasant grey building facing the sea. Tradition asserts that the Apostle's house stood opposite the Cathedral to west, where the Orphanage now is. This building was the residence of former Captains of San Thomé, hence the royal arms on the outer wall. Interest also attaches to another house in the High Road, namely the Seminary. Here St. Francis Xavier is believed to have lodged in the small upstairs room at present occupied by the Vicar-General, Mgr. A. M. Teixiera. Saint Francis arrived at San Thomé in April 1544, and remained for a period of four months. The yellow Church of St. Rita stands near the southern end of the town. Its eastern wall displays a tablet inscribed in Armenian characters, "In memory of the Armenian nation, 1729," the year in which the tomb of St. Thomas was reopened. During the early ages it owed its preservation to the Armenians, from whom the Portuguese learnt the tradition.

ADYAR.

After leaving San Thomé the road runs southward to Adyar. On the left lies the rifle range of the Madras Guards, I. D. F. To right, partially screened by trees, is the old white Portuguese Church of St. Lazarus. Beyond again, and hidden from sight, is the equally venerable Church of Mae de Deus. This the Jesuits were required to relinquish in 1775, when a Papal Bull, abolishing their order, reached the Portuguese Bishop of Mylapore. As the territory had previously been ceded by the Nawab of the Carnatic to the English Company, Father Lewis Costas appealed against the eviction to Governor Wynch of Madras. The big building overlooking the water on the right belongs to the Maharaja of Jeypore. Keeping to the left the main road soon reaches the Adyar, a tidal river spanned by a bridge about 520 yards long, completed in 1842 and named after Lord Elphinstone, at that time Governor of Madras. The large red building on the southern bank, is the Headquarters of the Theosophical Society, who own the adjoining property of two hundred and sixty-three acres. The grounds extend for nearly a mile along the river, and include a pleasant stretch of seashore. The picturesque white edifice, on the opposite bank, is Brodie Castle, a private residence named after James Brodie, who received a grant of the site in 1796. He was in the Company's employ as a Civil servant. In 1800 he was Garrison Storekeeper and was warned that either he must relinquish private trading, or resign. Two years afterwards he was drowned in the Adyar while boating.

The Theosophical Society dates from November, 1875. It was founded in the United States by an attorney known as Colonel Olcott, from his having fought in the Civil war of 1862-65. His object was to promote theological research and the investigation of psychic phenomena. All creeds were welcome to participate, in token of which the walls of the Convention Hall at Adyar bear representations of Sakya Muni, the historical Buddha, the Christ, Zoroaster and Krishna. Apparently Colonel Olcott's idea was very similar to that inspiring the Moghul Emperor Akbar (1566-1605), who instituted the celebrated Friday evening debates in the Ibadat Khana, or Hall of Worship at Fatehpur Sikri, near Agra. History records how the Great Moghul sat enthroned in the centre. Around him, from the encircling gallery, Jesuit missionary, Brahmin priest, Buddhist, Jain, Shiah, Sunni, Parsi, Jogi, Fakir and Sadhu propounded their beliefs and unbeliefs in heated controversy.

Three years after its inception the Theosophical Society removed its headquarters from New York to Bombay. In 1882 it established them at Adyar where, for £600, Colonel Olcott had purchased a house and 27 acres of ground then known as Huddleston Gardens. Since that time the two names most prominently associated with Theosophical propaganda have been those of Madam Blavatsky, a Russian, and Mrs. Besant. The former interested herself chiefly in psychic phenomena, confining her activities to attaining spiritual rather than temporal power.

Entrance to the Society's grounds is by an ordinary iron gate to left of the road. Soon the visitor passes under a sculptured trilithon, the stone posts of which are the spoils of a Hindu temple at Chandragiri, the capital of the last Vijianagar kings. Beyond is the Vasanta Press. To north is the library, a large red building, its outer wall decorated with raised elephant heads in white relief. Inside is the Convention Hall, containing a fine statue depicting Madam Blavatsky seated, with Colonel Olcott standing beside her. Possibly the feature of most interest to casual visitors to Adyar is the giant banyan tree, one of the largest in India. It grows in Blavatsky Gardens. It is said that three thousand people have assembled under its branches at a sitting. Picturesque, too, is the palm grove, where a bust of Colonel Olcott is enshrined on the site of his funeral pyre. The following is inscribed on the pediment:—

"Henry Steele Olcott, Colonel U. S. A. Army, President-Founder of the Theosophical Society. On this spot his body was given back to the elements, February 17th, 1907. May he soon return."

The memorial is surmounted by a cross about which a serpent is twined and stands on the bank of the river to east of Headquarters.

ELLIOT'S BEACH.

Blue sea, an uneven stretch of yellow sand strewn with red brick masonry remains, and a sombre background of casuarina trees. Such is Elliot's Beach about a mile and a half to south-east of Elphinstone Bridge. It is a favourite bathing resort, and likewise a popular place for moonlight picnics. It takes its name from Mr. Edward Elliot, a Justice of Sessions, who built himself a house there some time prior to 1837. The crumbling red brick foundations are all that survive of it. He was a son of the Hon'ble Hugh Elliot, Governor of Madras from 1814 to 1820.

SECOND DAY . . . . . ***Morning.***

Visit St. George's Cathedral, Teynampet, Agri-Horticultural Gardens, the Museum, Connemara Library and Victoria Technical Institute, Pantheon Road.

ST. GEORGE'S CATHEDRAL.

Large though it is St. George's Cathedral in Mount Road is dwarfed by its spacious compound, a flat and rather bare expanse, which seems to call for the scenic grouping of trees and flowers. The sacred pile is a stately yellow building, which, from a distance, owes its chief architectural distinction to lofty porticos supported by massive columns. Designed early in the last century by Colonel Caldwell, it was erected by Major Thomas Fiott de Haviland, of the Engineers, and was consecrated, on January 8th, 1816, by Bishop Middleton of Calcutta. In 1835 Madras was pronounced a separate diocese, and Daniel Corrie, LL.D., appointed the first Bishop. His ministration was brief. He died on February 5th, 1837, and was buried in the adjoining churchyard. A life-sized statue of him, in white marble, stands at the east end of the north aisle.

The interior of the Cathedral is white, and conveys an impression of light and space. Here again a double row of eighteen tall smooth pillars add greatly to the effect. The arched ceiling is beautifully decorated in raised plaster, and the small windows are filled in with stained glass. The Bishop's throne is of finely carved wood. A wealth of handsome historical monuments and mural tablets lines the walls. Immediately inside the main entrance is a fine group portraying Bishop Dealtry, obit 1861, ordaining two clergymen. Opposite to it is a monument, by Chantrey, to Doctor James Anderson, the Physician-General and famous naturalist, who died in 1809, and was buried in St. Mary's Cemetrey. He founded a botanical garden in Nungumbaukum, and another at Saidapet. The former site is now known as Pycroft's, and the latter as Lushington's Gardens. He introduced silkworm culture into India, likewise that of cochineal. The dried specimens of plants, which he sent to the British Museum, led to the founding of the National History Museum at South Kensington. Believed to have been of Swedish origin Doctor Anderson entered the Company's service at the siege of Manila, in 1672. His monument was the first

erected in the Cathedral, and his name is still the most distinguished in the medical annals of Fort St. George. Passing from the vestibule into the main aisle, the entrance is surmounted by the colours of the 8th Madras Infantry, and the Drum Major's staff inscribed with the date 1761. To right is the Bishop's vestry containing portraits of all the Bishops and Archdeacons of Madras.

Among the many handsome memorials lining the south wall, one of the most striking is a finely executed figure of Faith, by Flaxman, holding a book in her left hand and a long Latin cross in her right. This commemorates John Mousley, the first Archdeacon of Madras. Near it is another work by the same celebrated sculptor. This is a life-sized statue of James Stephen Lushington, second son of Sir Stephen Rumbold Lushington, Governor of Madras (1827-32), and grandson of General Harris, who commanded the army which captured Seringapatam in 1799.

Low down in the wall is a beautiful mosaic tablet depicting the Nativity. This is to the memory of Lady Ayling, wife of Sir Wm. Ayling, Judge of the High Court, Madras.

The revolving brass lectern, or "Eagle," is a memorial to George Warlow, M.A., ninth Archdeacon, obit January 25th, 1884. To south of the chancel steps is a marble bust of Bishop Gell, whose episcopate extended from 1861 to 1899. He bequeathed to the Diocese a valuable library of more than two thousand volumes, which are kept in the Archdeacon's office, a square grey building at the south-east corner of the compound, characterised by green shutters and a parapet encircled roof. On the north side of the sanctuary a brass tablet commemorates the wife of Lieut.-Colonel H. St. C. Carruthers, I.M.S. The latter donated a solid gold paten and chalice to the Cathedral. On the chalice is an inscription:—"To the glory of God and in memory of Minnie Alice Carruthers 1863—1904". It is further decorated with a cross and wreath of diamonds, once part of the jewellery of the deceased.

A splendid statue by Weeks occupies the east end of the north aisle, and portrays Bishop Corrie, founder of the Georgetown Grammar school, said to be the oldest purely educational establishment in the city. Nearby is a memorial to Norman Pogson, the distinguished astronomer and discoverer of twenty new variable stars, and ten minor planets. Attention is at once attracted by Chantrey's monument to Heber, second Bishop of Calcutta, author of many famous hymns, who died suddenly at Trichinopoly in 1826. Other important tablets are to Amelia Boileau, only child of Sir Frederick Adam, who commanded Adam's Brigade at Waterloo and was Governor of Madras from 1832 until 1837, to William Parry, obit 1824, founder of Parry and Company, and to Captain Samuel Best, F.R.S., to whom the Madras Presidency owes its comprehensive scheme of roads.

A UNIQUE RAILING.

The graveyard lies to north-east. Part of the encircling railing is unique of its kind, namely that bounding the old cemetery from the northern to the eastern gate. It is composed of musket barrels, bayonets, pikes and halberd heads. The lower line of railing consists of bayonets thrust into the barrels of horse pistols. Various theories exist concerning the origin of these weapons, which include eleven hundred muskets and an equal number of pikes and halberds, a thousand and fifty pistols and as many bayonets. One suggestion is that they belonged to the Madras Fusiliers, the sergeants of which regiment carried halberds on parade until 1857. General belief inclines to accept the statement that they were taken at the capture of Seringapatam in 1799. This view is strengthened by the name of V. Dubois, which is engraved upon them, it being a well-known fact that Tipu Sultan's Arsenal was in charge of Frenchmen. When the Cemetery was extended, in 1890, the new railing was carefully modelled in conformity with the old, nevertheless it requires only a very cursory examination to detect the difference.

The main entrance is a yellow gate house still known as the old bell tower. It consists of two square buildings united at the top by a white washed pavilion of octagonal shape surmounted by a dome. Immediately inside, to left, stands the lofty tomb of Lieut.-Colonel John Noble, obit July 17th, 1827, founder of the Corps of Horse Artillery on the Madras Establishment. The corners are marked by four six-pounder guns from his old Corps in lieu of pillars. His portrait was removed from the Artillery Mess at St. Thomas' Mount to the upper smoking room of the R. A. Mess, Woolwich, but a marble statue of him, by Chantrey, is still in the garrison church of St. Thomas.

A mitre and pastoral staff distinguish the resting place of Bishop Dealtry to whose energy the Cathedral owes its peal of bells.

Pathetically enough the first to be buried in the graveyard was Elizabeth de Haviland, née de Saumarez, wife of the Architect of the Cathedral. She died on March 14th, 1818. As her epitaph states:— "She stands first in the awful book and gives a date to the register." Her monument is of black Pallavaram granite, sometimes styled Charnockite from the fact that this stone was used for the construction of the Job Charnock memorial in Calcutta. Nearby sleeps Sir H. Levinge, P. C. S., who, by building Pamber House, at Kodaikanal, is regarded as having founded that hill station. Bishop Corrie and his wife sleep side by side under two big box-like cenotaphs of identical design.

AGRI-HORTICULTURAL GARDENS.

A side road divides the Cathedral from the Gardens planted by the Madras Agri-Horticultural Society in 1835. They cover about 22 acres and are romantically laid out with flower beds, tanks gay with lotus, glass houses, lawns and groves of trees. The botanical collection is varied and representative. On entering, the eye is caught by a small stone pavilion supported by pillars. Instinctively one looks for a statue, preferably Diana in view of the surroundings. It is disillusioning to learn from Ramalingam, the Head gardener, that the classical bower is an abandoned reservoir. Its roof supported a tank whence pipes supplied water for the fountains in the central pond. Special interest attaches to the great sausage tree near the Superintendent's office. Known scientifically as the *Kigelia pinnata*, or Madagascar Bignoniacea, it was the first of its kind to be introduced into India rather more than half a century ago. Since then its seedlings have been widely distributed. It instantly attracts attention by reason of its huge cucumber, or sausage shaped pods, and its clustering orchid-like flowers of a deep shade of red which hang straight down from the branches for several feet, on slender stems, hence its Tamil name of globe marrum. Nearby is a tall palm, the *Corypha umbraculifera*, or Thali Panay. From remote antiquity its leaves have been used for the writing of Mantras and Puranas. Flying foxes are partial to its fruit. Close to it is yet another sacred tree, the *Couronpita guianensis*, known in Tamil as Nagalingapu (snake lingam flower). Its blossoms are pink and open at night. During the day the petals fall off. The fruit is vivid green, hard and round, hence its common appellation of cannon ball tree.

The curious blossom curves forward after the manner of the expanded hood of a cobra, forming a canopy over a pistol shaped like Siva's emblem, the lingam. The flowers are offered at puja. The Saraga Indica is a large tree associated with the Ramayana. Under it Sita sat in the Asoka grove, when carried captive to Ceylon by Ravana. Then there is the *Ficus krishna* immortalised in the Mahabharata. When the god sported with the milkmaids at Mathura they filled its pitcher-like leaves with butter for him to eat.

The grounds are free to all. On week days they are open from 7 until 11 a.m. and again between 2 and 6 p.m. On Sunday the hours are the same except that the gates close at 5-30 p.m. The Nursery Garden is on the opposite side of Cathedral Road, a little to the east. Here seeds, growing plants and flowers may be bought. The Society charge a small membership fee. An annual show is held in February.

THE MUSEUM.

This is one of the handsomest and most interesting buildings of its kind in India. Madras may well be proud of it. The extensive grounds, in which it stands, once formed part of an estate of 43 acres granted to the well-known contractor, and civil servant, Mr. Hall Plumer, in 1778. He built the Assembly Rooms, styled the Pantheon, wherein society of those days disported themselves according to the fashion of the time. In 1789 he sold the place to a committee formed for the express purpose of promoting and organising the amusements of the settlement. A Master of Ceremonies was appointed, who directed many a brilliant ball, banquet and dramatic entertainment under its convivial roof. Mr. Moorat, an Armenian, purchased the property in 1821. Nine years later he disposed of it to Government. From then on it was styled the Collector's Cutchery until 1851, when it was converted into a museum, and was presented with a geological collection by the Madras Literary Society. Since then the old Pantheon has been extended and improved out of all recognition. It maintains its ancient tradition as a place of dramatic entertainment, by a theatre.

The contents of the Museum are admirably arranged. It is claimed that the collection of old brass gods is the finest in existence. Much of it was treasure trove. When the Muhammadan led armies of Golcondah, the Moghuls, Haider Ali, and Tipu Sultan, swept in devastating hordes over the land, Hindus naturally hastened to bury their Lares and Penates. together with the portable contents of their temples. These remained hidden in the earth and were, in many cases, forgotten, until the plough brought them to sight. The armour is particularly interesting and representative. Some of it was contributed by the Arsenal in the Fort. Archæologists will find much to study and admire, particularly some unique remains from the famous Buddhist ruins of Amaravati, which date back to the second century of our era. Among the relics is one of the utmost importance, as it is believed to be a bone of the Buddha himself.

CONNEMARA LIBRARY.

Named after that genial Governor of Madras, Lord Connemara (1886-1890), the Library adjoins the Museum and contains a large selection of works of reference. Visitors to the Reading Room should note the splendid marble statue of Lord Cornwallis, erected by public subscription in 1800, when it stood in the old Fort Square, and subsequently in a stone pavilion in front of the Secretariat, whence it was removed to its present position.

VICTORIA TECHNICAL INSTITUTE.

To those who imagine that the ancient Dravidian arts and industries of Southern India belong rather to the past. than the present, a visit to the Victoria Technical Institute, in the grounds of the museum, will be nothing short of a revelation. Here, in a noble hall, with marble floor, and walls and ceiling decorated with chunam—the shell plaster for which the Madras Presidency is famed—they will find objects of a beauty and excellence entitling them to a place of honour in a museum. The Institute has the additional charm, for the visitor, that he can possess himself of any of the exhibits at an extremely moderate price.

Particular interest attaches to those historical muslins and printed calicoes which, in turn, drew Portuguese, Dutch, British, Danish, and French to establish settlements on the Coromandel Coast. The colouring and designs are sumptuous. Curtains, table cloths, palampores and bedspreads introduce elaborate scenes from the great Indian epics, as well as conventional patterns handed down with traditional fidelity from remote antiquity. Saidapet produces a variety of its own, being a quarter long associated with the industry. The cotton is first treated with a preparation of buffalo milk, after which the design is stamped on with a wooden block and coloured with a pen, or else with melted wax.

Silk weaving is represented by gorgeous saris and scarves, many of which are interwoven with gold after the manner of the celebrated kincobs of Ahmedabad. Very fine Madras embroideries, the speciality of Muhammadan men workers, take the form of table cloths, dresses, d'oyleys, handkerchief, etc. The gold and silver do not tarnish when washed. Jewellery, brass, copper, ivory and wooden figures, boxes and trays, rugs, carpets, and mats, lacquer work, real lace, cane tables and chairs, and splendidly carved furniture all testify to the fact that, far from being extinct, the indigenous arts and crafts of the Presidency can achieve as excellent effects to-day as at any time during their long and glorious history.

The Technical Institute is modern. It was established in order to bring the local specialist into direct touch with the general public, to the greater benefit of both. On January 26th, 1906, the foundation stone was laid by the King-Emperor George V. at that time Prince of Wales. Public subscriptions partially defrayed the cost of the building, the Hall being a memorial to the Queen Empress Victoria. Mr. Henry Irwin, C.I.E., drew the design, skilfully adapting the Moghul style of Northern India to modern requirements. The pink Tada sandstone, in which it is carried out, is a happy substitute for the red sandstone of Fatehpur Sikri, wherewith the Great Moghuls constructed their palaces.

SECOND DAY.—*Afternoon.*

Drive out to the Little Mount. Visit the Apostle's Cave, the cross in the rock, and the miraculous spring. Proceed through Guindy to St. Thomas Mount.

MOUNT ROAD.

Romantically situated on the further bank of the Adyar the Little Mount is one of the three famous places in Madras associated with the Apostle Thomas. It is reached by Mount Road, the celebrated thoroughfare completed in 1795, which connects Fort St.

George with the military cantonment of St. Thomas' Mount, 8 miles to south-west The entire route is of interest. Starting from Wallajah Bridge, in the north, it traverses the Island. To left lie the golf course, polo ground and Gymkhana Club. Further on is Government House. Close by is the spot on which Lawrence's force attempted to make a stand on December 11th, 1758, and prevent the French passing up Mount Road and so into Black Town. They were driven from the position on the following day, and compelled to withdraw into the Fort, whereupon Count Lally encamped his army in Government House Garden, and the plain by Turing's house nearby.

For a while the road is lined with important shops, hotels and other imposing edifices. Gradually these dwindle in size and merge into a bazaar. Then comes more open ground, and those spacious compounds for which the city is renowned. A big house to left is the residence of the Rajah of Bobbili. Soon the highway traverses the district known as a "Thousand Lights." Here curiosity is aroused by the name, and also by the large and sombre red mansion at the corner of Peter's Road. Popular tradition ascribes it to Umdat-ul-Umrah, the ninth Nawab of the Carnatic (1795-1801), who owned extensive property in the neighbourhood. On the opposite side of the way is a white Muhammadan mosque. Then follow St. George's Cathedral on the left, and the Agri-Horticultural Gardens. These are shortly succeeded by another bazaar. Trees line the way, mostly banyans. The Long Tank lies on the right behind a mud embankment fringed with palms. Beside its waters Lord Cornwallis inspected the Bengal Detachment on January 28th, 1791, and conferred with General Medows prior to marching upon Bangalore and Seringapatam. A start was made on February 9th. The army consisted of 18,000 combatants and ten times as many followers.

To left the Military Grass Farm stretches southward to meet the Veterinary Hospital, Saidapet. On the opposite side is a curious stone monument topped by a granite knob, and further characterised by yellow corner pilasters and a red base. Its outer face bears the following inscription :—

"This bridge, erected as public benefit from a legacy bestowed by Mr. Adrian Fourbeck, a merchant of Madras, is a memorial, useful as lasting, of the good citizen's munificent liberality. It was erected by his executors, T. Pelling, I. De Fries and P. Bodkin from the plan, and under the direction of Lt.-Colonel Patrick Ross, Chief

Engineer, in the year of Our Lord, 1786." The inscription is repeated on the other three sides in Latin, Telugu and Urdu.

Fourbeck's bridge spans a drainage channel crossing Mount Road from the Long Tank. Behind the monument lie Lushington Gardens, now the residence of the Collector of Chingleput. In a map of 1837 the site is named General Campbell's, or Botanical Gardens. Earlier still it was known as the Honourable Company's Nopalry, from experiments carried out there by the Physician General and famous naturalist, Doctor James Anderson, in connection with the cochineal industry. The insects were fed upon the nopal shrub specially imported from Mexico for the purpose.

The majority of garden houses bordering Mount Road date from the 18th century. They were erected by the Company's servants, who were anxious to escape inland from the congested area of White Town, and the hot glare of the sun and the sea, and so eagerly sought to obtain grants of land in the Choultry Plain, as it was then termed. This embraced the villages of Numgumbaukum, Teynampetta and Reyapetta, and extended from the Triplicane-San Thomé Road on the east, to the Long Tank in the west. A good idea of the extent of the Company's territory in the 18th century is conveyed in a proposition, put forward in 1775, to define the limits of Madras by surrounding it with a bound hedge composed of palmeiras, bamboo, calderas, milk bush, prickly thorn, etc., from "the redoubt at San Thomé along the borders of the San Thomé River," *i.e.* now the Adyar, "to Morse's Choultry, through the Long Tank, round the village of Chetput, the Octagon and Vepery, and from thence to be continued to the sea at about a mile distant from the northern wall of Black Town," This suggestion was referred to Colonel Ross, the Chief Engineer, who approved it. Orders were issued for the hedge to be marked out. At the same time, the Committee of Revenue were instructed to ascertain the nature of the soil, the value of it and the owners thereof. Apparently the plan never materialised. It was again put forward by Mr. Stephen Popham eleven years later.

MARMALONG BRIDGE.

To left rise the gleaming white buildings of the Teachers' College, Saidapet. Almost immediately the yellow posts of Marmalong Bridge flash into sight. Each is marked with a raised white cross,

and surmounted by a ribbed, melon-shaped ornament. It takes its name from the neighbouring village of Mambalam, and was built in 1726, by Petrus Uscan, an Armenian merchant from Manila; hence the inscription at its northern end :—"Hunc pontem edificari jussit pro bono publico Caja Petrus Uscan, natione Armeni anno salutis MDCCXXVI." He died on January 15th, 1751, aged 70, and was buried in his own chapel at Vepery, the site of which is now occupied by St. Mathias' Church, where his tomb may be seen in the graveyard near the main entrance to the sanctuary. He left a fund for the maintenance of his bridge.

Below, on the northern bank of the Adyar, the ground is gay with a bright and varied display of clothing spread out to dry in the hot sunshins. The scene presented by the dhobi ghat is typically Indian. Washermen bend over the river, beating wearing apparel, and houshold linen upon the boulders, with a splendid disregard of consequences.

THE LITTLE MOUNT.

To south of the bridge a side road, on the left, runs through the village of Marmalong, situated on the river bank just below the Little Mount, where the Apostle sought refuge in a cave when driven from Mylapore. The hillock is a picturesque mass of grey rock softened by the green of trees, above which rise gleaming white buildings and red-tiled roofs. The scarped sides are partially girdled by a buttressed wall. Steps lead up the northern face. At their foot is a stone cross engraved with Armenian characters. It is said to commemorate the son of a wealthy Armenian merchant who, in 1612, built the northern extension of the Church, easily distinguished from the older portion, which has a bomb-proof roof, and is altogether more substantial.

A good description of the place is given by a Jesuit father named Desideri, who, in 1726, was sent to Rome with despatches from the Bishop of Mylapore. There Father Desideri wrote a report of his eastern travels, from which the fellowing is an extract :—"The Little Mount, when in its natural condition, was nothing but a most rugged and inaccessible pinnacle of rock. About the year 1551 it was first made easier of approach, and levelled in places for the convenience of pilgrims, according to a record made for the benefit of posterity on a stone standing at the stair towards the north of the hill. Here was built the Church of the Holy Virgin, given to the Portuguese Fathers of the Society of Jesus, who afterwards erected a sort of hermitage on the peak of the rock, and the Church of the Resurrection, where exists the stone cross cut in low relief."

The first flight of steps leads to an artificially levelled platform paved with gravestones. Here stands the Church of Our Lady of Health. Entering by the north door the eye is caught by a roughly carved granite slab let into the smooth white wall to left. Cut on it is a figure of St. Thomas, staff in hand, and the date 1612. Beyond lies the older bomb-proof portion of the sanctuary, terminating in a long flight of steps ascending to the altar. On the left is a mural tablet inscribed:—"The cave, where lay hid, persecuted just before being martyred by Raja Mahadevan, King of Mylapuram, A. D. 68, Thomas, one of the twelve, the great apostle of India, the very one who put his fingers into the wounds of his Lord and God." Here the verger brings candle and matches. Bending double he precedes the visiter downstairs into the celebrated cave. On the wall, to left of the low doorway, a cross is cut in the rock. The ground is uneven and the atmosphere close, and charged with the stifling odour of bats. A beautiful little marble altar occupies the east end. To south a narrow crevice in the rock is the aperture through which St. Thomas is believed to have escaped when wounded at his devotions by a lance thrust.

Writing in 1646, de Rezende states:—"On the Little Mount, where he lived, is a house of prayer, with a hole in the rock through which the Saint escaped when his life was attempted. All around are carved crosses on the rocks. These are places deeply venerated even by the heathen, who bring hither oil and rice of the first fruits. The sovereign of the land is a heathen known as the King of Vijianagar."

Leaving the Church by the west door a short walk leads to more steps. These ascend to another levelled platform, where the Jesuits erected their small church of the Resurrection, above a cross cut in the rock near the ground to the east. This is believed to have been the altar before which the Apostle celebrated mass. Above it is a second cross of stone coated with whitewash. The first is said to have sweated copiously, and been veiled with clouds whenever misfortune threatened the Portuguese nation. Close by is a small white domed building. This shelters the miraculous spring. Tradition asserts that in the time of the Apostle there was no Adyar river ; consequently the multitudes, who flocked to hear him preach, suffered greatly for want of water. Moved by their distress, St. Thomas fell on his knees and prayed, then struck the rock with his staff. "Immediately there gushed forth a spring of clear water, possessing the power of healing diseases when drunk with faith in the intercession of the Saint. Up to the present time the Hindus continue to visit the place and drink this water. Christians, laymen as well as priests, are persuaded, and testify that the water still performs the most marvellous cures." Father Desideri, S.J., 1726.

Higher still is the hermitage built by the Jesuits, now occupied by the parish priest, the Rev. A. S. Nunes. The roof commands an extensive panorama. Immediately below, to north-west, the rocks are dominated by a small white-domed building. This marks the spot where St. Thomas stood when preaching. Beyond lies Marmalong, its white houses embowered in trees, and its name a corruption of the Tamil Ma-ambalam, or place of mangoes. The population once included a number of weavers. It is on record that the wealthy Armenian, Shamier Sultan, received a grant of land there in 1767. Most of his printed calicoes were manufactured in the village. On September 13th, 1781, General Sir Hector Monro's army encamped at Marmalong, on their return from the disastrous campaign against Haider Ali, which resulted in the capture of Colonel Baillie, and the annihilation of his detachment, on the ill-fated field of Perambore.

To south-west the large red building near by is the old gaol, now the Sub-Registrar's Office. Further still are the Engineering College Works. Most imposing of all is Government House, a great white edifice standing in an extensive park. This was the hot-weather residence of the Governors of Madras prior to the annual April exodus to Ootacamund, which came into vogue about half a century ago. The suggestion emanated from Sir William Dennison (Governor 1861-66). It found favour with his successors in office ; hence a Government House was established in the Nilgiris in 1879.

For a long time the Little Mount formed part of extensive church lands. As late as 1803 an official record defines these as extending from Sydah Pettah Road on the north, to Venkatapooram Road on the south, and from Vengadapooram Garden on the east to the bridge on the west "containing in the whole." The place is mentioned in the writings of all early European travellers, several of whom describe miraculous phenomena witnessed in connection with the rock-cut cross. Now holy sites are not the draw which they used to be. The Monte Pequene of Manucci's "Storia do Mogor" is apt to be somewhat deserted.

ST. THOMAS' MOUNT.

From the southern end of Marmalong Bridge the road to St. Thomas' Mount turns sharply to right. It passes a terra cotta coloured pavilion containing a statue of the King-Emperor George V. To left lies an old garden house now converted into Oakes' Cigar and Cigarette Factory. A little further on stretch the combined golf and race course, where a pathetic memento stands near an old masonry pillar on the eastern boundary. It consists of an upright slab of smooth grey marble inscribed:—"Erected to the memory of Excelsior, by his trainer who loved him. He won seven races and was killed on the course, on October 12th, 1897, when going strong and well, and likely to win his eighth." On the far side of the ground, to west, is another monument, a curious white obelisk that tapers from a massive base to a point. Four grey walls encircle it and it bears the lines:—"Erected to the memory of Major Donald Mackay, who died September 27th, 1783, and was buried underneath, in front of the lines of the Army."

Soon afterwards the road reaches an open plain. This is the parade ground. Near the northern corner is a domed pavilion of graceful pillars and a white funeral urn. About it runs a circular grey wall. The monument commemorates Colonel Samuel Dalrymple, R. A., one of three gallant brothers, all of whom took part in the storming of Seringapatam in 1799. A family tradition claims that Kirby, the eldest of the trio, cut down Tipu Sultan at the Water Gate of his captal, where the body of that redoubtable leader was subsequently identified among a heap of slain. In proof of the assertion a sword is preserved, which Kirby is said to have taken from Tipu Sultan. The brothers were natives of Haddingtonshire, where their adventures inspired the local toast:—"Here's to Kirby, Hew and Sam and may they take Seringapatam!"

St. Thomas Mount early became a popular resort with English settlers at Fort St. George. Near the north-eastern base of the hill they built some dozen garden houses. These were destroyed by the French in 1758-9. In one of them Manucci resided and entertained Daud Khan, the second Nawab of the Carnatic. Here Major Caillaud and Captain Achilles Preston inflicted a defeat upon the French, on February 9th, 1759.

THE ASCENT.

A neat little village lies at the northern foot of the Great Mount. Midway, along the narrow street, a side track strikes left to a high grey and white gate of four simulated arches, and a square central door surmounted by a cross, and the date 1547. Within is a brick pavement, and several flat gravestones bearing old Portuguese inscriptions. Steps, flanked by low grey walls lined with seats, lead upwards. Petrus Uscan, the Armenian merchant who built Marmalong Bridge, likewise donated this stairway. Small grey shrines appear at intervals, characterised by recesses for lights. The lowest, on the left, is said to mark the spot where the famous painting of the Madonna and child, attributed to St. Luke, was found. The picture is on wood and is now in the Church above. Many miracles are attributed to it.

Goats and sheep browse on the hill side amid a wilderness of rock and cactus. To right, near the summit, is a species of hastily constructed fort. The walls are about 3 feet high, and consist of roughly hewn stone so arranged as to leave gaps for gun emplacements. It commands the road to Poonamallee.

The top of the hill is a level platform paved with red brick. Above it rises the Church of Our Lady of the Immaculate Conception. Armorial bearings appear over the door. Within, on the right, is a small side altar. Here may be seen the painting of the Mother and Child. Pious belief asserts it to be one of seven portraits executed by the hand of the Apostle Luke. St. Thomas, it is claimed, brought it with him to India. A Russian connoisseur, an authority upon the origin and manufacture of ikons, identifies the picture as 11th century Cretan. A mysterious stone of a curious black colour is let into the wall above. This is the world-famous bleeding cross discovered by the Portuguese deeply embedded in the ground. They were told it was engraved on the face of the rock, and that St. Thomas was kneeling in front of it praying, when a Brahmin dealt him a death thrust with a spear. Rusty fragments of a blood-stained weapon of the kind were found near by. Nevertheless, Marco Polo (A. D. 1254-1324) quotes a current belief that the Apostle was accidentally killed on the Mount, by the arrow of a fowler.

A great sensation was caused at Goa in 1507, when travellers from the Coromandel Coast brought word that the Apostle Thomas had suffered martyrdom on a hill near the ancient Hindu city of Mylapore. Don Francisce di Almeida was Vicéroy at the time. He promptly despatched four messengers to investigate and verify the rumour. Two died on the journey. The report brought back by the survivors was forwarded to the King of Portugal. On Corpus Christi Day, 1521, a party of Portuguese set out from Pulicat, about 24 miles north of Madras, to visit the Mount of the Apostle. They found a very old Church with naves and aisles. Timber pillars supported the roof. The sacristy was covered by a dome and dwarf spire. Peacocks and crosses formed the decoration. A small chapel nearby was said to be the mausoleum of a Hindu prince, whom the Apostle had converted. They started excavating, and found the reputed remains of a Raja styled Tani Mudalyar, and a stone whereon was engraved:—"I give one-tenth of income from trade both by sea and land to this holy shrine, so long as sun and moon endure. I enjoin my descendants to maintain it on pain of malediction." Repairs were effected, and a monastery and other buildings established. Correa describes how, in 1540, Manuel de Gama was despatched to San Thomé to bring away the Portuguese, and dismantle the town and the Church of the Apostle. Seven years later further excavations on the Mount led to the discovery of a stone cross bearing an unintelligible inscription, spotted with what appeared to be blood stains. On the strength of this the Portuguese erected the Church to Our Lady on the site of the find, and sunk the carved stone into the wall above a small side altar, where it is now an object of universal interest. Faria Sousa gives the following account of it:—"The chapel being repaired and beautified in the year 1551, the stone was solemnly set upon it. At the time the priest pronounced those words of the gospel 'Missus est Angelus Gabriel,' it began to change colour and became black and shining, then, sweating, turned to its own colour plainly discovering the spots of blood which, before, were obscure."

The late celebrated epigraphist, Doctor Burnell, attributed the sculpture to the 8th century A.D. He identified the inscription as Pehlvi and translated it:—"In punishment by the cross the suffering of this, the true Christ, and God above, and Guide for ever pure."

Correa tells how a beacon fire was lighted nightly on the Mount, for the benefit of mariners, who no sooner sighted it than they struck their sails and made obeisance.

Dr. Fryer wrote of the neighbourhood in the latter half of the 18th century:—" St. Thomas, his Mount, is famous for his sepulture and for a tree called Arbor Tristis " (the Arabian Jasmine) " which withers in the day and blossoms at night. About this Mount live a caste of people, whose legs are as big as those of elephants, a judgment on them as the generation of the assassins of the blessed Apostle St. Thomas."

The pulpit is remarkable for its decorations. These introduce mermaids gaily painted and lavishly gilt. On the wall behind is a crudely painted picture of Our Lord, the eyes of which seem to follow the spectator wherever he moves. The floor is partially paved with gravestones, under one of which sleeps the donor of the pulpit.

PANORAMA.

As the Mount is the only elevation for some miles it naturally commands an extensive panorama. Steps on its western side lead down to a small square cemetery enclosed by walls. Beyond rises a low hill known as Monkey Mount. Thereafter the tree dotted plain stretches to Poonamallee, now a convalescent station for British troops, about 14 miles south-west of Madras. The town was ceded to the Company by Muhammad Ali, eighth Nawab of the Carnatic (1749-1795). Prior to that it had played a role in history as the headquarters of a Naik, or Governor, and boasted a fort of some strength and a mint. For the first few years of its existence the English settlement at Madras was subject to Poonamallee. As such it suffered much annoyance from the exactions of successive Governors, both Hindu and Muhammadan. Two large Hindu Temples and a handsome Mosque still bear testimony to the former greatness of the place. A large red brick hospital occupies the site of the Old Fort.

To south-east of the plain a brief range of hills rises above the abandoned cantonment of Pallavaram. The highest peak is crowned by a white Muhammadan tomb and Mosque, a favourite place of pilgrimage at the Bara Wafat festival, held on the anniversary of the Prophet's death. The range has been freely quarried for the far-famed

Pallavaram gneiss, or Charnockite, from which the historical buildings in Madras are constructed, notably Pitt's Pillars erected in 1732, and the recent harbour works. Below, in the cantonment, Colonel J. M. Coombs, Commandant of the Station, was murdered in 1833 by a Havildar, who mistook him for another officer. Previous to that Coombs had a narrow escape during the mutiny at Vellore, when he owed his preservation to hiding under a washtub. A couple of miles further on is Chromepet celebrated for the large leather factory of that name. From there the road runs on to Chingleput, whence a side track branches east to Seven Pagodas, the ancient Pallava sea port, world-famed for its unique archæological wonders, in the shape of rock cut temples, galleries, rathas, and sculptured boulders.

In a straight line to north-east of the Mount lie the Little Mount, where the Apostle dwelt in a cave, and Mylapore Cathedral, containing his grave. Immediately below, at the foot of the hill, is the parade ground ringed round with officers' houses, the grey garrison Church of St. Thomas, and the great white Artillery Mess, once considered the finest in India, and now used by Infantry. Other buildings are occupied by the Ordnance, Barracks and a hospital.

THIRD DAY.........*Morning.*

Visit the Zoological-Gardens, People's Park, Moore Market and Evening Bazaar.

ZOOLOGICAL GARDENS.

Situated in the People's Park the Zoological Gardens may be visited for the modest entrance fee of six pies, otherwise half an anna. They contain an admirable collection of birds and animals. The grounds are charmingly laid out with ornamental water fringed by flowering trees, beneath the green shade of which solemn storks promenade with that majestic gait to which they have bequeathed their name.

Under the old Vijianagar sovereigns the place was an elephant garden. These animals were an essential adjunct of royalty, moreover they constituted one of the four branches of all ancient Hindu armies, *vis.*, Elephants, Chariots, Cavalry, and Infantry. The garden was still in existence when the English founded Fort St

George in the 17th century. Its memory survives in the present Elephant Gate, and the road leading thereto.

At Christmas an annual fair is usually held in the People's Park and continues for about ten days.

MOORE MARKET.

It would be difficult to imagine a more noisy, or characteristic scene than that presented by the large general market named after Lt.-Colonel Sir George Moore, K.C.B., one time President of the Madras Municipality. Despite much opposition, Colonel Moore succeeded in abolishing the old insanitary bazaar in George Town, and substituting the present imposing red structure designed by Mr. R. E. Ellis, Municipal Engineer. The cost of erection was estimated at three lakhs of rupees. Quadrangular in shape the edifice consists of outer verandahs and inner galleries erected about a central court open to the sky. The south side is practically devoted to bird fanciers and animal dealers. Booksellers congregate along the northern verandah, where the wary, and persistent are occasionally rewarded by the discovery of a rare first edition. Vegetable stalls, butchers, and vendors of every sort and description are well represented in other parts of the market.

EVENING BAZAAR.

Despite the nocturnal suggestion of its name this crowded thoroughfare is literally patronised at all hours of the day. It enjoys a reputation throughout India for its beads. These range from the carved wooden rosaries affected by the religious, to those imitation pearls, coral, gilt and coloured beads wherewith, faute de mieux, the fair of all ages and climes have ever sought to enhance their charms.

Other important marts are the Parchery Bazaar, in North George Town, the Kotwal Bazaar noted for its fruits and vegetables, and the Mundy Bazaar, which specialises in rice both "boiled" and "raw."

THIRD DAY.........*Afternoon.*

Visit the ancient Parthasaradhi Temple at Triplicane, the great Mylapore Temple and Tank, and the Luz Church. Return via Mowbray Road.

PARTHASARADHI TEMPLE, TRIPLICANE.

The famous Parthasaradhi temple is one of the oldest and most revered Hindu strongholds in Southern India. Special significance attaches to it from the fact that it is the only one dedicated to Vishnu under his title of Parthasaradhi, divine chariot driver to Arjuna, chief of the five Pandu Princes, and hero of the Mahabbharata.

During his ninth human incarnation Vishnu was known as Krishna, in which mortal form he contracted a warm friendship with Arjuna. It was this friendship that led the god to act as chariot driver to the prince at the epoch closing battle on the plain of Kuru-chet, near Delhi. Krishna, on that occasion, uttered the inspired lines of the Bhagavat Gita, or Book of Divine Wisdom. When hostilities had ceased Krishna journeyed southwards until he reached the spot now covered by his temple. Here he took up his abode and elected to be worshipped as Parthasaradhi, the Chariot Driver. Historians ascribe the war of the Mahabbharata to the 15th century B.C. Local tradition attributes far greater antiquity to the shrine, and especially to the sacred tank nearby. It also claims that, at the period when the temple was founded, the present crowded district of Triplicane was practically uninhabited. Instead it was dotted with plentiful pools of water gay with floating lilies, hence its correct name of Tirualli-kani, or the "Place of Beautiful Lotus Tanks". These have all been gradually filled in and built over with houses. A notable exception is the large masonry reservoir of many steps, to east of the shrine. It is long and narrow in shape. An ornamental pavilion of striped red and white pillars, and a white gopuram, as the pyramidal roof is termed, rises island-like from the midst of its placid green water. Shrines overlook the west bank, and a towering processional car painted brightest crimson, and crowded with the carved figures of rearing horses and divinities.

Entrance to the temple is by way of a mantapam, or stone hall, covered by a flat roof, its corners marked by winged figures of Garuda, the kite god, the vehicle of Vishnu on which that powerful divinity rides. At the east end of the hall a large elephant invariably attracts a crowd of spectators. The animal is young, and is a particularly fine specimen of its kind. It was presented to the shrine by Karlekar, the well-known circus proprietor. Passing through a door, under a towering gopuram, a courtyard is reached. Beyond again a long narrow gallery intervenes between the portal, and the sanctum sanctorum. When the lights are lit at sunset it is possible to discern the god, a majestic stone figure of imposing height, erect and grasping a sword. Those privileged to draw near describe the face as deeply pitted by the arrows aimed at Arjuna's chariot during the great battle of the Mahabharata.

Much sanctity accrues to the temple from the praise lavished upon it by the sacred Vishnuvite poets of old time, notably Pai Auluvar, believed to have flourished 3012 B. C., Thirumayasai Auluvar and Thirumangai Auluvar. Mention of it occurs frequently in the Nalayara Prabhandam, or Book of Four Thousand Hymns, many of which are earlier than the Christian era.

A net-work of buildings extends behind the sanctuary to west. Among them are shops where sacred figures are sold, and brightly coloured and gilt holy pictures painted after the style of ikons. Most of the faces of the people, in the immediate vicinity, display a large white V intersected by a vertical red line, between the brows. This is the Vishnu mark and denotes their sect.

The temple is the scene of several brilliant annual celebrations, particularly the floating festival in February-March. Small effigies, of the god and goddess, composed of the five auspicious metals, are carried in state to a brilliantly illuminated barge, in which they make the tour of the lake seven times, while musicians play and Dasis, or nautch dance girl before them. The great car festival is in April.

The tank is known as Kairavani Tirtham. Its waters are held to possess the miraculous virtue of cleansing from sin all those who devoutly perform their ablutions therein. The Sthala Purana extols it as the holiest of all holy waters, and avers that a single bath in the sacred Kairavani or Lotus Tank, is more effective than a thousand in the River Ganges. Little wonder that it attracts many pilgrims.

On more than one occasion the Parthasaradhi Temple has been converted to military purposes. In March 1673 the French, who were then masters of San Thome, garrisoned it strongly in anticipation of a fresh Muhammadan attack, the withdrawal of the Golcondah army being regarded as a mere temporary measure of the kind significantly expressed as "reculer pour mieux sauter." Governor Langhorne protested unavailingly. In 1676 the Sultan of Golcondah to whom the territory belonged, had issued a kaul leasing Triplicane

Photo by Lt.-Col. H. A. Newell.

to the merchants. This was sanctioned by Nawab Sayyid Musa in 1792, who agreed to accept an annual quit rent of Pagodas 65. During their second siege of San Thomé the Dutch made Triplicane their base.

MYLAPORE TEMPLE.

The great Dravidian temple at Mylapore is a still better example of the curious architectural style characteristic of the Madras Presidency, to which it is, practically, confined. The sanctuary is dedicated to Siva, the second person of the Hindu Trimurti, or Divine Triad, of which Brahma is the first and Vishnu the third. To west lies a large and beautiful quadrangular tank completely covered with lotus. A picturesque red and white pavilion rises from the centre. Stone steps line the banks of the tirtham, which are fringed with stately palms excepting where, to west, a great pipal tree casts its protecting shade over a stone platform, whereon are grouped nagakals, or carved cobra tablets, votive offerings from women desirous of sons. A high wall, alternately striped red and white, stretches along the further bank. Midway it is pierced by a much decorated white gopuram. Behind rises yet another, and very much loftier pyramidal doorway, coloured red and brown. Lesser towers spring up around.

Mylapore derives its name from a legend to the effect that Parvati, the divine consort of the presiding deity of the temple, here worshipped Siva who appeared to her in the form of a peacock, hence the place was ever after known as the Peacock Town. The temple was built at a very early date by the ancient Chola Kings. Mention of it occurs in many old hymns. Saint Thirugyanasambantha Swamigal sang of it. Local historians assign him to the seventeenth century B. C. They further state that divine wisdom was vouchsafed him at the precocious age of three, and tell how he resuscitated the dead bones of a man named Sivanasi Chettiar, transforming them into a beautiful living girl. Other sacred authors born at Mylapore were Nicruvaluvar, of immortal fame, and Vaysia Nayanar.

THE LUZ CHURCH.

Although doubt has been cast upon the authenticity of the date A. D. 1516, carved above its door, the Luz Church is generally admitted to be the oldest Christian sanctuary in Madras. Situated in

Mylapore it lies inland about a mile to west of San Thomé Cathedral, whence it is reached by Rosary Church Road. Tradition ascribes its origin to a miracle. Early in the 16th century some Portuguese mariners were in danger of being shipwrecked during a gale off the coast. They had lost their bearings and vowed a Church to Our Lady if she would assist them. Instantly a guiding light flashed out enabling them to steer safely ashore. Once landed they followed the illumination, until it was abruptly extinguished on the site where they subsequently erected the Luz, or Church of the Light. The annual festival is held on the first Sunday after the 5th August, that day being sacred to Our Blessed Lady of Snows. The sailors built their sanctuary outside the fortifications of San Thomé, at a little distance beyond the city wall, the great west gate of which stood in Rosary Church Road. That the Luz was held in universal veneration is proved by its constant mention in the writings of early travellers.

Time has dealt kindly with the old sanctuary. It lies a little to west of the high road behind a faded pink wall, weather stained and patterned with moss. Four steps lead up to the green wooden gate. This admits to a quaint and ancient enclosure grass grown and paved with a few gravestones, some resplendent with armorial bearings, and others displaying Tamil inscriptions. One of the earliest is dated 1637. To south flaming yellow poppies illuminate a picturesque grey stone grotto enshrining Our Lady. This was blessed on August 19th, 1917, and commemorates the fourth centenary of the Church. To west, sharply defined against green palms and blue sky, stands the Church of the Light, the oldest in Madras, as testified to by the date A.D. 1516 carved above its door. The architectural style is not without a certain distinction, and is that peculiar to Portuguese and Spanish Mission Churches of the period. The interior walls are white. There are several handsome memorial tablets, many of which are dedicated to members of the one time influential de Fries family. A small upper gallery extends across the east end. The arched roof is tinted grey and reveals raised white comets grouped about a central sun. Over the altar the ceiling is more extraordinary still, with its cherub and seraphin heads, many coloured figures in relievo, crossed arms, stars, planets, vases and angels holding aloft what appears to be a large green and white sugar-coated cake. The high altar is a massive wooden erection painted white and heavily overlaid with gold leaf. It is surmounted by figures of the Madonna and Child wearing tall 16th century crowns. The two side altars are similar in style. That to north is dedicated to Saint Joseph, and the other to Saint Anthony. Both are represented by very beautiful old ivory figures carved in Portugal. Outside the south wall, near the west end of the Church, is a tablet inscribed:—

"Fra Pedro da Atousia, Religios Obserte de S. Francisco Edificio esta Igreja de Nossa Senhora da Luz E.M. 1516."

On the same side, overlooking a brick paved court, and the Priest's house, steps lead up to the belfry on the roof of the Church. Originally there were three bells. Of the two which remain, one is dated A.D. 1806. The grave yard lies to north. It is dominated by a slender wooden cross mounted on a high masonry base of pyramidal form. A similar cross and pedestal occupied a site to north-east of the Church, in close proximity to a Brahmin residence, the inhabitants of which strongly objected to it. In deference to their wishes it was removed in April 1918, and the materials used to erect the modern cross now situated immediately in front of the east gate.

In 1782, when strong reinforcements of the King's troops arrived in Madras, the 23rd Dragoons were quartered at the Luz. An infantry detachment was cantoned in San Thomé, various ecclesiastical buildings being requisitioned as barracks. This drew forth a protest from the Governor of Goa, who wrote requesting that the troops quartered in the Churches of San Thomé might be accommodated elsewhere.

MOUBRAY ROAD.

This has been described as the most beautiful road in Madras. As late as 1798 it was merely a cart track, traversing country chiefly under wet cultivation. It takes its name from Mr. George Moubray, Government Accountant, who arrived in Madras in 1771. He acquired 105 acres of land in the neighbourhood, at a rental of Pagodas 80. Here he built a house in turn known as Moubray's Cupola and Moubray's Gardens. The property is now occupied by the Adyar Club.

SOME OTHER PLACES OF INTEREST.

ROSARY CHURCH.

Built by the Portuguese, in 1635, the Rosary Church stands on the northern side of the ancient thoroughfare now known by its name. Originally it was inside the city walls of old San Thomé. It is a characteristic yellow missionary building of the period. The facade introduces pilasters, and an arched window above the entrance. Large ornamental urns decorate the roof, the further end of which is dome crowned, beneath a cross. The interior is beautifully kept by the nuns, who maintain a constant supply of fresh flowers. The high altar is of handsomely carved wood work, as is the reredos enshrining the Madonna.

Manucci recounts a dramatic episode, in connection with the Rosary Church, which occurred in 1704. At that time the city was subject to the Muhammadans. A new Chief Captain had been despatched from Goa to command the Portuguese at San Thomé. His name was Nuno Silvestro Frade. He failed to pay the usual ceremonial call upon the Mussulman Governor, Mir Usman, nor did he ask permission before erecting a hundred godowns, and preparing a quantity of gunpowder. The Muhammadans made no sign of resentment. They waited until October 5th, to retaliate, when they interrupted the procession of the Rosary Mass, seized the candles, scoffed loudly, knocked against the banners and portable shrines, and seated themselves on the altar steps, smoking and laughing. Discomfited the Portuguese left the Church and retired to their homes. At this Mir Usman repaired to the house of the new Portuguese Commander. Imagining that it was a visit of ceremony Frade came out to receive him, whereupon he was seized and an attempt made to drag him off to prison. Joa Rebello, President of the Rosary, attacked the Muhammadan guard, firing and killing the trooper in charge of Frade. Rebello was instantly slain. A riot ensued under cover of which Frade escaped, ultimately finding refuge in the house of a poor widow, who alone would take him in.

THE OBSERVATORY.

Madras Observatory is the Greenwich of India. Situated in College Road, Nungambaukum, it occupies an extensive compound on the right bank of the River Cooum. It is a large red building picked out with yellow. Twin white domes and a wind gauge occupy the flat roof. At 3-58 P.M. daily the telegraph wires are cleared, and Madras flashes the correct time all over India exactly on the stroke of 4 o'clock.

The city owes its Observatory to Michael Topping, Astronomer and Surveyor, who advanced the project in 1789. In his report he laid stress upon the number of valuable astronomical instruments in the Presidency, and the urgent need to provide suitable accommodation for them. Sanction being obtained from the Company, Mr. Edward Garrow's house on the plain was purchased for Pagodas 5,000. This was converted into a residence and office for the astronomer. A further sum of Pagodas 2,462 was expended upon erecting the Observatory, which was pronounced complete in 1792.

Prior to this astronomical observations had been carried on privately by Mr. William Petrie, who entered the Madras Civil Service in 1765, and built his own local observatory.

MADRAS LITERARY SOCIETY.

Near neighbour is the Madras Literary Society, a branch of the Royal Asiatic Society. The various activities of the Society include a splendid lending library containing some seventy thousand volumes. Resident members pay a quarterly subscription of Rs. 10. Those desiring to join for a brief period only can do so at Rs. 4 per mensem.

ST. MARY'S CEMETERY.

St. Mary's Cemetery dates from 1761. It occupies the north-west angle of the Island, where it lies on the south side of Body Guard Road near the Central Railway Station. When, in 1758, the French made a second attempt to capture Fort St. George, they found valuable cover in the old English burial ground, crowded with immense masonry monuments, which stood on the site now appropriated by the Law College. After the enemy had withdrawn, it was decided that military interests necessitated the demolition of the Black Town graveyard and mausolea. In 1760 the Vestry applied for a new burial ground. This was granted them. Two years later a wall was erected round the Campo Santo at Government expense, and it received the name by which it is still known.

Many of the graves are of historical interest, notably one bearing the modest inscription :—"Nicholas Morse Esq., once Governor of Fort St. George, aged 72 years."

Nicholas Morse assumed office as Governor of Madras, on January 17th, 1744. Two and a half years later the city surrendered to the French, under de la Bourdonnais, who undertook to accept a ransom. This agreement was repudiated by Dupleix. Governor Morse was carried off to Pondicherry, eventually exchanged and sent to England. Afterwards he returned to Madras, where he lived in retirement until his death on May 8th, 1772. He was a direct descendant of Cromwell, through the Protector's daughter, Bridget Ireton.

Another tomb, dated 13th June 1795, marks the resting place of Stephen Popham, Solicitor to the Company, who, in 1782, obtained permission to reclaim a marshy tract between Muthialpetta and Peddanaikpetta, and build houses thereon. Such was the origin of the busy and important thoroughfare now known as Popham's Broadway, leading out of China Bazaar Road. St. Patrick's Catholic Cemetery lies to north-west of St. Mary's. On the opposite side of the way is St. Andrews' burial ground, belonging to the Scottish Kirk.

BODY GUARD LINES.

These adjoin St. Mary's Cemetery, whence they extend eastwards to Government House Bridge. Although the early Governors of Fort St. George appeared in public accompanied by guards and an impressive retinue, the Body Guard does not seem to have been organised as a cavalry escort until the outbreak of hostilities with Haider Ali in 1780. In that year Governor Whitehill directed the Town Major to raise a mounted Indian Force. This was known as the Governor's Troop, and consisted of one Jemadar, two Havildars, two Naiks, a farrier and twenty privates, armed and equipped from the Company's stores. Horses were provided by various gentlemen of Madras. The Nawab of the Carnatic contributed saddles, holsters and bridles. The troop was furnished with carbines. Four troopers invariably rode beside the Governor's carriage. On other occasions the entire force acted as escort. In January 1781 the Body Guard saw active service, when it participated with two complete Companies of Sepoys, a hundred Poligars and two light guns, in clearing the neighbourhood of straggling parties of the enemy.

In 1788 the Body Guard was increased to a Lieutenant, two Cornets, one Subhadar, two Jemadars, four Havildars, four Naiks, a Vakil, a farrier, two drummers and trumpeters, and fifty troopers. At the same time it was supplemented by a company of Indian Infantry.

The present strength of the Body Guard is seventy men commanded by a Captain, a Resildar and a Jemadar. More than half the force is composed of Muhammadans.

The Nawabs of the Carnatic had their own Body Guards, as had their elder sons.

POWDER MILLS.

Notwithstanding its two tall chimneys nothing could be less like the modern conception of a factory than the drowsy old world pleasaunce at Perambore, still known as the Powder Mills. It dates from the latter part of the 18th century, and is enclosed by low walls, and shaded by a variety of trees, conspicuous amid which is the great Baobab (Adansonia digitala) from Senegal, its huge suede covered pods filled with a variety of tamarind greedily devoured by squirrels. Entrance is through a gate to south. The interior contains numerous godowns, a number of widely separated bombproof buildings, and some large masonry tanks, where big pink lotus float upon opaque green water. To north a broken stone bridge partly spans a channel. Originally it led to a widespread bombproof edifice, over the arched door of which is the sign "Government Fisheries." When powder ceased to be manufactured at the Mills the place was converted into the Government Harness and Saddle Factory, now transferred to Jubbulpore.

An earlier powder mill stood on the island. From the description of it preserved in old records it appears to have been built on much the same plan as the one still standing in Perambore. A later powder mill was erected to north-west of the island. This was destroyed by the French in 1746. Yet another was constructed in Egmore from the materials of the Capuchin Church of St. Andrews in Fort St. George, demolished after the restoration of Madras in 1749. The Egmore powder mills were blown up by the French in 1759. In 1770 it was decided to build powder mills immediately to west of the Seven Wells, on the site afterwards occupied by the Mint.

SALT COTAURS.

Cotaur signifies shed. The name Salt Cotaurs applies to the district to west of the People's Park, where the Madras and Southern Mahratta Railway have erected extensive godowns near Elephant Gate Road. This tract was formerly waste land chiefly occupied by salt pits, pans and salt cotaurs, which last were used for storing salt collected in the neighbourhood, as well as large supplies brought in by barges from Ennore, Pulicat, etc. Under the East India Company the salt industry was farmed out to contractors. This led to abuses. Early in the 18th century Rayasami Papaiya, Chief Dubash to the Governor, was deprived of his high rank and confidential post for creating a corner in salt. He was reinstated by Governor Hastings in 1720. Now salt is a Government monopoly controlled by that branch of the Revenue Department exclusively devoted to Salt and Abkari.

SEVEN WELLS.

The picturesque title of Seven Wells applies to a large-walled enclosure at the further end of Mint Street, planted with mango trees and overlooked on one side by a line of godowns belonging to the Public Works Department. As a matter of fact, the compound contains ten covered wells. These once yielded 300,000 gallons of water daily. Now only two are working, and supply 80,000 gallons per diem to Fort St. George. Puffs of smoke, and the noise of machinery come from a small yellow power house in the middle, its activity attested by great cinder heaps piled up in the background. An old storage reservoir, of quaint and massive design, dominates the north-east corner at a high level.

In the early days of the English settlement at Madras much inconvenience was experienced owing to lack of reliable water. The nearest obtainable was at Seven Wells, two miles distant from the Fort. It was fetched in casks and transported by the scavenger in conservancy carts. A scheme to convey the water by aqueducts, or other means, was advanced by Captain George Baker in 1771, and approved by the Company. The ensuing contract specified that Baker should provide the Fort with sufficient good and wholesome water to last a garrison of six thousand men for not less than four months, at the rate of three quarts a day per head. Baker was to defray the cost of constructing the works, but was to receive a monthly salary of Pagodas 200. His contract was to run for twenty-one years. Additional payment was to be made for all water supplied to the factory and buildings, shipping and town of Madras. Delay was experienced in obtaining lead for the pipes, which did not arrive until May 1778, nevertheless Baker was as good as his word, and delivery of water to the Fort began two months later.

As some of the wells stood in private property compensation was awarded the owners. Subsequently the Company erected an 8-foot wall some 920 yards in extent, entered by a gateway to west.

PACHAIYAPPA'S COLLEGE.

Madras is justly proud of this famous institution, which it owes to the posthumous generosity of Pachaiyappa Mudaliar, a celebrated Dubash in the East India Company's Service. The College stands on the west side of China Bazaar Road, whence it looks across the Ordnance Lines and playground of the Law College, to Fort St. George and the sea. It is an imposing building, its lower storey yellow, and its upper white, dignified by a deep, pillared portico of classical design.

Pachaiyappa, its founder, had a romantic career. He was born in the sacred city of Conjeeveram in 1754, several months after the death of his father, an event which plunged his mother in poverty. When her orphan son was five years old the poor widow moved to Madras. Here she was befriended by Powney Narayana Pillai, a powerful dubash, or interpreter, in the Company's service, who took charge of Pachaiyappa's education. The lad was also taught English, a particularly profitable accomplishment at that period. He was naturally clever. This, and his patron's influence caused him to make rapid headway. He began his commercial career as an agent. From this he rose to be dubash, next Revenue Farmer and Commissariat Contractor. In 1788 Sir Archibald Campbell, then Governor of Madras, entrusted him with a financial mission to the Raja of Tanjore. Pachaiyappa had already proved his diplomatic ability in negotiations with Haider Ali, Tipu Sultan and other heads of states during the wars of the Carnatic. When at Kumbakonam, in 1794, he made a will by which he bequeathed most of his large fortune to the service of Siva and Krishna, fate having denied him a son. The residue was to be divided among various religious and educational establishments and gifts to the poor. He died at Tiruvaiyar, in the Tanjore district, on March 31st, 1794. His executors failed to carry out the provisions of his will, and misappropriated the funds, until the matter was brought to the notice of Sir Herbert Compton, then Advocate-General. The case came up before the Supreme Court, when it was found that most of the money had been dissipated. Finally, owing to the exertions of Mr. George Norton, the next Advocate-General, a certain sum was recovered, chiefly in the form of jewels, the sale of which realised eight lakhs. Nine Hindu trustees were nominated to carry out the provisions of the will. Under their directions a primary school was established in Madras in 1842, and called Pachaiyappa's Central Institution. Here instruction was provided free. As the number of students soon became overwhelming, the trustees found themselves compelled to charge a small monthly fee, which came into force in 1849. Meantime, on October 2nd, 1846, Mr. Norton had laid the foundation stone of the present College, which was formally opened by the Governor of Madras, Sir Henry Pottinger, in 1850. As recently as 1915 the Government presented the College with a playground at Chetput. A chair of Mathematics was established in 1904, and one of Physics in 1913. It is a hopeful sign of the times that the College is awakening to the importance of technical education, and its bearing upon the future status of India not only in the Empire, but the world. Other educational establishments, founded with funds bequeathed by Pachaiyappa, consist of a school at Conjeeveram, his nativë city, and another at Chidambaram.

MEMORIAL HALL.

Erected by public subscription the Memorial Hall commemorates the eventful year 1857, when the storm of mutiny, which swept over Northern India, left Madras unscathed. It is a massive building and stands near the Central Railway Station, and opposite the Medical College.

ST. ANDREW'S KIRK.

The tall yellow spire of St. Andrew's Kirk is 165 feet high. It constitutes one of the most familiar land marks in Madras. Situated due east of Egmore Railway Station the Church is surrounded by a big bare compound. The main entrance faces west, and consists of a deep classical porch supported by twelve lofty and very massive fluted columns topped by Greek capitals. Beyond lies an octagonal vestibule with a shallow domed roof. In the middle of the floor a round black marble tablet bears an inscription stating that the building was erected by Major T. F. de Havilland of the Engineers. The foundation stone was laid on April 6th, 1818, and Divine Service first held on February 25th, 1821. Among the mural monuments is a bust of John Wylie, M. D., Physician-General of Madras, obit 16th May, 1859. The inscription states that Doctor Wylie took part in the heroic defence of Coregaum, near Poona, on New Year's Day, 1818, when a small force of eight hundred, commanded by Captain Staunton, repulsed repeated attacks of the Peshwas' Army, numbering over twenty thousand.

The interior of the Church is circular. The handsome mahogany pews are curved in conformity with the general effect. Twelve tall Ionic pillars form a ring under a lofty central dome coloured a deep shade of emerald. Small stained glass windows, set high in the white walls, temper the outer glare to a dim religious light. The floor is paved with black and white marble. Major de Havilland, the architect, also constructed St. George's Cathedral, from designs drawn by Colonel Caldwell. Further works associated with his name are the old sea wall, Madras, and the curious rainbow arch at Seringapatam. Born at Guernsey, he was the son of Sir Peter de Havilland. Upon retiring he lived in his native island until his death at the venerable age of ninety.

MADRAS GUARDS.

The Headquarters of the Madras Guards are situated in a big white edifice north of St. Andrews' Kirk. The Corps dates from July 2nd, 1857. It boasts the proud distinction of being the sole survivor of those volunteer organisations raised, in various parts of India, under the stress of the Sepoy Mutiny. Lord Harris was Governor of Fort St. George at the time. He gave every encouragement to the new regiment, and was frequently present at parade, finally becoming Honorary Colonel-in-Chief in 1859, a precedent which has been followed by succeeding Governors. Colonel A. C. Silver was appointed to raise and organise the infantry, which mustered 536 strong on the Island, a week after enrolment, to receive arms, ammunition and accoutrements. Each man was given a fusil, twenty rounds of ball ammunition, a bayonet, belt and pouch. The cavalry numbered 95. They were served with swords and belts.

The establishment of the Cavalry was fixed at 100, and the Infantry at 700, exclusive of officers. The uniform sanctioned for the Cavalry consisted of a dark blue cloth tunic, single breasted, piped with red and elaborately laced with gold across the chest and down the seams. The breeches were of white buckskin, and were supplemented by high Napoleon boots, while the helmet was of red felt, with a gold chinstrap and device, the whole surmounted by a flowing white horse plume. The Infantry uniform was somewhat similar, excepting that white trousers, and a spiked white helmet were worn.

In January, 1858, Colonel Silver received permission to form a Rifle Company, the distinguishing uniform of which was green, with belt and pouch of black patent leather and a shako. On the 10th May of the same year the Madras Guards were presented with their colours. A public holiday was declared in honour of the event. The ceremony included the blessing of the colours by the Rev. F. G. Lugard, Chaplain of Vepery, and was a very brilliant and imposing one.

A detachment of the Madras Guards was present at Delhi on January 1st, 1877, when Queen Victoria was proclaimed Empress of India. A year later Government proposed the formation of an Artillery Company in Madras. The twenty-fifth anniversary of the regiment was celebrated by the officers presenting a silver shield to be competed for annually by rifle teams of the various companies. In 1906 the Guards took part in the annual shooting competition at Bisley, where they were represented by Major W. D. Smith, the present Officer Commanding the Regiment since the death of Lieut.-Colonel H. W. Gillman, I.C.S., in 1918. Major W. D. Smith's connection with the Guards dates from 1899. In 1914 he organised and took to England the "All-India Bisley Team," for which he received the congratulations and thanks of the Viceroy, the Commander-in-Chief, etc.

During the late world war the Madras Guards were partly mobilised and incorporated in the Indian Defence Force. As such a detachment was stationed at Fort St. George. Needless to say their bright uniforms are things of the past, the all enveloping khaki having descended upon them as upon the rest of the Army. Nevertheless the Madras Guards maintain their ancient privilege, unique among volunteers of wearing gold lace.

No mention of the Madras Guards, however brief, should omit the popular band which adds so much to the gaiety of the city. It was originally taken over from the 8th Light Cavalry by Colonel Silver in 1857, since when it has shared in the honourable record of the Madras Guards, whose motto is "Ready, aye ready." The March-past is to the lively strains of "The Old Irish Washerwoman."

ST. MATTHIAS' CHURCH.

From the weather stained appearance of its yellow walls the picturesque and interesting Church of St. Matthias, in Vepery, appears to be very much older than is really the case. This impression is accentuated by the dates borne by the curious eighteenth century tombs in the grave-yard. Their presence is explained by the fact that the existing edifice occupies the site of a private chapel dedicated to Nossa Senhora da Milogres, built by the well-known Armenian merchant, Petrus Uscan, who, in 1726, constructed and endowed the Marmalong Bridge over the Adyar, near the Little Mount, and the steps leading up the Great Mount.

Petrus Uscan lies buried in front of St. Matthias' Church. His grave is almost in a straight line due west of the main door, and consists of a large flat slab of granite surrounded by an ornamental scroll border. At the head appear a pair of skulls and the usual cross bones. Below is his name, also the date, January 15th, 1751, on which he died at the age of seventy. A longer inscription, in Armenian, gives the name of his father, Coja Uscan, and of his grandfather, Coja Pogose of Jalfa, near Ispahan.

When the French restored Madras to the English in 1749, the British Admiral received instructions to confiscate all Capuchin Churches in the neighbourhood, under suspicion of the priests having helped the enemy in 1746. Petrus Uscan was notified, as his chapel had been served by Father Severini, a member of the proscribed order. The Danish Missionaries, Fabricius and Breithaupt, immediately applied for the Vepery Chapel stating their desire to utilise it for the Society for the Propagation of Christian Knowledge. Petrus Uscan protested. It was then decided that the chapel should remain vacant, pending instructions from the Company. A verdict was received in favour of the Danish missionaries, consequently the building was handed over to them in 1752. Meanwhile Petrus Uscan had died. His executors produced a will wherein he expressed a desire to be buried in the chapel at Vepery, which he bequeathed to Father Severini. Ultimately, in 1770, compensation was awarded the Capuchins in lieu of the chapel. In 1782 British troops were quartered in the Church and were alleged to have damaged it extensively. Soon afterwards Fabricius became involved in considerable financial difficulties and even spent two years in the debtors' jail, from which he was rescued shortly prior to his death. He, too, is buried in the graveyard, but the spot is not marked.

The vestibule displays a square granite tablet let into the red brick pavement. It bears an inscription stating that the foundation stone of the Church was laid on December 8th, 1823. It was built by the Society for Promoting Christian Knowledge at the wish of Bishop Middleton, first Primate of Calcutta. The Honorable East India Company contributed towards the expenses. John Law was the Architect, and a collection of Madras coins, current at the period, was deposited under the foundation stone.

NEIGHBOURING PLACES OF INTEREST.

ENNORE.

Ennore is a popular week-end resort with those partial to fishing, boating and bathing. Its name is derived from two Tamil words signifying "Eel" and "Village," and is now an elastic term including the neighbouring hamlet of Kathiavakam. The quickest and most direct route is by road, via the ancient village of Tiruvottiyur, famed for a large Dravidian temple of much sanctity. Ennore can also be reached by rail, or by the Buckingham Canal, a distance of some eleven miles. Visitors possessing neither house boats, nor villas, find accommodation on the lakeside, in a furnished bungalow belonging to Mr. Nurse, of the Madras Stable Company. They must, however, provide their own food. The Fisheries own another bungalow near by. The locality is celebrated for oysters and salt. The latter is considered the best in India.

PULICAT.

Pulicat lies 12 miles north of Ennore on the Buckingham Canal. Historically it is of interest as the first place on the Coromandel Coast to be colonised by Holland. The Dutch East India Company founded a factory here in 1609, protecting it with a fort still known as Castle Geldria. Under them it rose to be a rich and prosperous seaport carrying on a considerable trade with the Straits Settlements, notably Penang. It was a famous market for jewels, and also for cotton goods, particularly chintz. The English obtained permission to establish a factory at Pulicat in 1621, but abandoned the attempt in the following year owing to the hostility of their neighbours, upon whom they avenged themselves in July 1781 by seizing the fort, factory and dependencies. These were restored to Holland four years later. Pulicat surrendered to the English in 1795, and was not given back to the Dutch until 1818. Ultimately it became an integral part of the British possessions in 1824. Time and warfare have obliterated most of its former glories. Dutch rule is commemorated, appropriately enough, by the graveyard. The men of Holland attached the greatest importance to their tombs, some of which are very fine examples of carving.

Pulicat Lake is 37 miles in extent. The original name of the place is Pazhavailcaud, a combination of Tamil words meaning the "old acacia forest." It boasts a traveller's bungalow.

RED HILLS.

The title of Red Hills is a distinct misnomer as applied to the flat district surrounding the large tank which, since 1870, has provided Madras with its principal water supply. Mountains there are but at such a distance as to appear cloud-like against the horizon. The reservoir is 10 miles north-west of the city. It connects, with the Cholavaram tank, whence a channel flows 8 miles to an anicut across the Corteliaur, a river draining an area of 137 square miles. Both the tanks were excavated many centuries ago. They have been enlarged and strengthened since their appropriation as city water works. The two bungalows on the bank belong respectively to the Municipality and P.W.D., to one or other of whom application must be made before either can be occupied.

Under the ancient Pallava dynasty the neighbourhood included a military station. A fortress stood near Pozhalore, a village bearing a Tamil name signifying a "hollow." The stronghold was the headquarters of one of the governors of the twenty-four cottams, or provinces, into which the Tondaimandalam country was divided. He presided over the surrounding district, which now contains the city of Madras. Kovil Madavaram, the local name of the Red Hills, was distinguished for a large Buddhist temple and another to Siva. When the Pallavas were overthrown the Siva sanctuary at Kovil-Madavaram was robbed of its bronze doors, which were carried off to Tanjore.

COVELONG.

Tradition avers that Covelong, the old Dutch settlement some 20 miles south of Madras, was once a large and flourishing metropolis, 10 miles in extent. Comalammah was the presiding goddess. In those days the place bore the high sounding Sanskrit title of Nityakalyanapura, or the Daily Marriage City, as well as its more prosaic Tamil name derived from Kovalam, a headland. It is reached by a side track that strikes east from the Chingleput trunk road near the small railway station of Vandalur.

The Dutch erected a fort and factory at Covelong about 1612. The place was held sacred by Muhammadans, owing to a legend that the body of a holy man was washed ashore there in a chest, whereon was engraved the request that it might be accorded burial. A tomb was duly erected. During the rule of Saudud-ullah-Khan, Nawab of the Carnatic (1710-32) a Mosque was built in honour of the mysterious remains. In 1745 Nawab Anwar-ud-Din erected a fort, and changed the name of the place to Sandat Bunder or Auspicious Port. The French occupied Covelong in 1750. Two years later Clive forced them to surrender, whereupon he blew up the fortifications totally destroying those of the Dutch.

CHINGLEPUT.

Chingleput, the Lotus Town, is 36 miles S.-W. of Madras. A pretty local legend attributes its foundation to a chieftain who, grief distracted at the death of his beautiful wife, dreamed that he heard a voice command him to collect her ashes and place them in an earthenware pot. This accomplished he was to wander the world until such time as lotus should burst in full bloom from the vessel upon its touching the ground near a lake. Early records assign the place to the Pallavas, one of the ancient ruling dynasties of Tondaimandalam, the country embracing the Coromandel Coast in the first centuries of our era. From the Pallavas Chingleput passed to the Western Gangas of Mysore and then to the Cholas. In the 14th century it was absorbed by the rapidly extending Vijianagar Empire.

the power of which was broken by the combined Muhammadan Sultans of the Deccan at the battle of Talikottah, in 1565. Chingleput became the head-quarters of Timma Raja, a relative of the vanquished Hindu dynasty. The Fort dates from him. One of his successors granted the site of Fort St. George, Madras, to the English. The French stormed Chingleput in 1751. A year later it was captured by Clive. Lally neglected to reduce it before marching against Madras in 1758, an error which proved fatal to the success of his campaign. Now the old stronghold serves as a Reformatory, where troublesome boys are converted into useful members of society. The town possesses a Travellers' bungalow, a railway refreshment room, some cave temples and various other objects of interest.

SEVEN PAGODAS.

Known to Europeans as Seven Pagodas the ancient Pallava sea port of Mahabalipuram is 17 miles from Chingleput, the nearest railway station, and 52 miles from Madras, whence it can be reached by the Buckingham Canal. Application for boats should be made to the Wharf Superintendent, the Basin, Madras.

After leaving Chingleput the road is flat and winding. Midway it passes a ridge, the highest peak crowned by an ancient Siva temple. This soars above the village of Tirukkalukundram and is known as the Hill of the Sacred Kites, from two of those birds, which fly there regularly at 11 o'clock every morning to be fed. Pious belief affirms them to be the spirits of two Brahman saints, sons of Kasiparasi, a Benares ascetic. Many centuries ago these holy men gained emancipation from the flesh at Tirukkalikundram. They are further credited with bathing daily in the Ganges and with passing the night on the sacred Island of Rameswaram. The goddess is styled Chokkanayagi and the god Vedagirisvara. The latter is here worshipped as special patron of the Vedas, which inspired works he is held to have transformed into the four mountain peaks, the highest of which supports his shrine. The Sthalapurana mentions the temple as having been endowed by both Chola and Pandyan kings. Once a Jain sanctuary it was known as Pacshitirtham, and as the Bird Convent.

Seven Pagodas owes its European nickname to a maritime tradition that seven temples, roofed with burnished copper, once extended seawards in a long line. Locally it is still believed to have been the capital of Mahabali, the demon king outwitted by Vishnu in his Vamana Avatar, or Dwarf incarnation. The correct name of the sea port is Mahamallapuram, the City of Mahalla, one of the numerous titles borne by the Pallava sovereign Narasimhavarman I., whose reign dates from about 600 A. D.

The place is world famed for its unique archæological remains in the form of monolithic shrines, notably the five rathas, rock cut galleries, sculptured boulders and the wonderful carved cliff styled Arjuna's penance. There is a Travellers' Bungalow, but visitors must bring their own supplies.

N.B.—"Seven Pagodas, Chingleput and Conjeeveram," an illustrated guide, by Lieut.-Col. H. A. Newell. Price Annas Eight.

SADRAS.

Just before reaching the village of Tirukkalikundram the road from Chingleput to Seven Pagodas splits into a fork. The right branch runs 9 miles to the quaint and picturesque Dutch seaport of Sadras. The old fort is in a ruinate condition with the exception of the graveyard of the nobility. This lies immediately inside the west curtain to south of the entrance, and contains some beautifully carved and characteristic tombs. Other interesting remains are those of the Dutch Governor's Residence and his Garden House overlooking a spacious and beautiful masonry tank. Both buildings are now as effectually hidden in jungle as was ever the enchanted castle of the Sleeping Princess. Under Holland the place was of commercial importance, and was particularly famed for its fine muslins. The English captured it in 1765 but it did not become an integral part of the British possessions until 1824.

Under the Pallavas it was a military station hence its name Shatturangapattanam embodying the four essential branches of an ancient Hindu army, viz., cavalry, infantry, elephants and chariots.

The inspection bungalow is sparingly furnished.

CONJEEVERAM.

Conjeeveram, or Kanchipuram, the glittering city, is 40 miles south-west of Madras. In the early centuries of our era it was the capital of the Pallavas, a dynasty which had a bull for a crest and a club for standard. They maintained their power until the 8th century when they were overthrown by the Chalukyas. Finally in the 13th century they disappeared from history.

Conjeeveram is one of the original Seven sacred cities of the Hindus, ranking second only to Benares. It abounds in temples, many of which are of immense historical and archæological interest, their inscriptions having afforded much valuable and unsuspected information. In the 7th century it was a Buddhist stronghold. As such it was visited by the Chinese pilgrim Hiuen Tsang. He described it as containing some hundreds of Sangharamas, and ten thousand priests, who studied the teachings of the Sthavera School belonging to the Great Vehicle. At one time many of the inhabitants professed the Jain faith.

Among Hindus it is popularly believed to have been the spot chosen by the great Trimurti—Brahma, Siva and Vishnu—for the celebration of their nuptials. Conjeeveram is on the railway.

CHIEF CLUBS.

Madras Club, Royapettah, established 1831.

Gymkhana Club, the Island, Mount Road.

Madras Cricket Club, Wallajah Road, Chepauk.

Adyar Club.

Madras Boat Club, Adyar.

Sailing Club. Anchorage and Boat Shed at Springhaven, the Harbour.

The Garden Club, Ottershaw, Marshalls Road, Egmore.

Cosmopolitan Club, Mount Road.

Trades Union Club, Cooum Boat House, Mount Road.

EARLY HISTORY.

According to Professor Haeckel the cradle of mankind was situated in the continent of Lemuria, long sunk beneath the Indian Ocean. Geologists have advanced the startling theory that what is now known as Dravidia, the generic term applied to the Madras Presidency, was connected with this submerged world, and was not included in Asia until some three thousand years ago. From man's birthplace in Lemuria issued that great branch of the human family scientifically classed as true Malay, variations of which are the straight-haired Mongols and the curly-headed Euplocami. It is claimed that the last survive remarkably true to type in the Dravidian population of Southern India and Ceylon, who are said to differ least from the primeval stock. Those who have changed the most, during the process of evolution, owe the fact to their having migrated furthest from their country of origin. Such is the case with the Euplocami settled in Europe where, at an early date in the history of civilisation, the Graeco-Italo-Celtic group attained a degree of intellectual, and artistic preeminence that has been the wonder of succeeding generations.

The country round about the present city of Madras was known to antiquity as Tondaimandalam, from Tandy, a "shrub," and mandalam, a "kingdom." Another name for it was Valanaud or "Extensive District," while the earliest Aryan emigrants from the north styled it the Dandaca Desert. It covered an area of 18,302 square miles. An old Tamil poet determines its boundaries in verse as :—" The Cheyar to the south, the sacrd Vengadam to the north, the everlasting sea to the east, and, to west, the desirable Mountains of the Bull. That this is the position of the Tonday country all are agreed."

The Cheyar River has been identified as the Chennaur or Yenaud. Vengadam is one of the many titles borne by the sacred hill crowned by the celebrated Tripatty Temple. The Mountains of the Bull constitute the range dominated by the old fort of Nandidroog, which earned such sinister notoriety during the Company's wars with Haider Ali and Tipu Sultan.

The first recorded inhabitants were the Korumbers, a pastoral tribe of Chola descent. Gradually these nomad shepherds diminished in numbers, and were replaced by the Vellaulars, described as an agricultural people consisting of three distinct branches. Under them the district came to be noted as " the excellent Tonday country, with clear watered fields, possessing learned men." Moreover it boasted " one thousand nine hundred townships beautified by palm trees."

For purposes of administration the territory was divided up into twenty-four cottams, each of which was ruled by a chief, who resided in a fort. In addition there were seventy-nine sub-divisions, styled nadus, the prototypes of the modern taluk. What is now the city of Madras was included in the Nazar nadu of Puzel Cottem, the fort of which was 10 miles to north-west at Kovil Mathavaram. (Red Hills).

The absence of definite dates renders the early chronology of South India largely a matter of conjecture. Of the four ages, or periods, into which it is broadly divided by its own historians, the three first belong to the dawn of the world and survive only in fable. The Dravidians are presumed to be direct descendants of an early people found in the cradle of humanity, which the learned place in that forgotten continent sunk deep below the rolling waters of the Indian Ocean. Geology and natural science alike point to the fact that the Dravidian country was at no very distant epoch separated from the remainder of Asia. The Sanskrit Puranic writers, Ceylon Buddhists, and local traditions all agree as to a tremendous seismatic disturbance at the southern point of the peninsula now divided from Ceylon by the Gulf of Manaar and Palk Straits. Nor is this the only evidence. The Buddhist Chronicles of the Cingalese record a great deluge B. C. 2387. European theologians place the flood at approximately 2348 B.C., from which it would appear that somewhere about that period considerable changes took place in the earth's surface.

Human remains, and other traces of primitive man discovered on the east coast, strengthen the theory that the Dravidians are indigenous to Southern India. Their language is unique and is far older than Sanskrit. Their religion consisted in worshipping the spirits of the dead, and included propitiatory ceremonies and offerings to demons, and more especially demonesses. The order of priesthood was unknown. The approved system of Government was monarchical, and definite areas of rule prevailed Their peculiar architectural style stands alone, and their temples are the largest in the world. Although they produced innumerable poets they were also a practical people and skilled in a variety of handicrafts, notably carving, sculpture, dyeing and weaving. Egyptian mummies, dating from 2000 B.C., have been found wrapped in fine Indian muslins. Silver, gold, pearls and precious stones were plentiful. The Dravidians evolved two alphabets, and two distinct classes of written characters, of which one was known as Vatterzhoot, or "round," and the other as Kelozhoot, or "vertical." They wrote on thin slips of wood, or palm leaves, a threaded bundle of which formed a book. Polyandry was practised and it was no uncommon thing for Queens to rule.

THE ARYANS.

It is not known when the first Aryans penetrated to Southern India. The earliest emigrants were probably religious ascetics and hermits, stragglers from that great band who, at the beginning of the Kali-Yuga, some 3000 B. C., left their home near the source of the Oxus in the vicinity of Bokhara, to cross the Indus and settle in the Punjab, on a strip of land about 60 miles long and 20 miles broad. Among the few who adventured as far as Dravidia the first to acquire fame was Agastya. He settled at the Court of the Pandyan king, adopted the customs and language of that nation, and compiled the first Tamil Grammar. Tamil is the oldest, richest and best organised of the Dravidian languages, and is commonly spoken throughout the districts from a few miles north of Madras, down to the extreme south of the Peninsula. It possesses two dialects. Of these Shen Tamil (meaning "perfection") is the most ancient and is the classical tongue of poetry. Coodum, or, "rude" Tamil is used in ordinary parlance. Dravidian literature is extremely prolific. Its poets are subject to certain curious rules. The alphabet consists of propitious and unpropitious letters. A poem must always begin with one of the former. Tradition records how a king was once killed by a poem addressed to him that started off with an unlucky letter.

With the Aryans originated that hereditary system to which the Portuguese applied the name of casta, or caste, to express those social distinctions which determined a man's calling in life, and ordained that a son should follow his father's profession from generation to generation.

In the beginning the most respected members of the Aryan community were the Rishis, who composed the hymns, but who belonged to no special class. Gradually grades were organised, until all mankind was rigidly catalogued. The first rank in this strange new order was assigned to the Brahmins, or priestly caste who, at the moment of creation, were believed to have issued from the head of Brahma. The Sanskrit equivalent of caste is varna, colour. That of the Brahmins was white. Their business in life was the performance of tremendous sacrifices calling for elaborate and complicated ritual, the least infringement of which would call down divine vengeance upon the luckless offender. Their mission was also to recite and interpret the Vedas, expound the laws and be the counsellors of Kings. The first portion of a Brahmin's life was to be spent in study, and in serving the master whose disciple he was. The second was to be lived with his wife. During this period he was to preach, instruct and assist at sacrifices "clean and decent, his hair and beard clipped, his passions subdued, his dress white, his body pure, carrying a staff and a copy of the Vedas, and wearing bright golden rings in his ears." The third and last part of his life must be spent in retirement as an anchorite until his spirit "quits the body as a bird leaves the branch of a tree at will."

The Kshatriyas, or ruling caste followed. Their colour was red, and they sprang from the arms of Brahma.

Next came the Veisyas, or traders, to whom yellow and brown were assigned. They were created from the thighs of Brahma and might indulge in commerce and agriculture.

Last of all were the Sudras, the black race who, as emanating from the feet of the God, were apportioned the task of serving the three upper classes. They might never acquire property, but it was forbidden to use them as slaves. All who did not come under one or other of these four categories were pariahs, or outcasts.

The caste system received a decided check under Buddhism. Missionaries of that denomination reached South India in the 3rd century B. C. and made many converts. It was, however, finally stamped out in the 8th century A. D. Jainism was practically extinguished in this part of the Peninsula at about the same time. A great Hindu revival followed. The 11th century was remarkable for the building of a number of Siva temples. Numerous shrines to Vishnu were erected in the 13th century.

HINDUS.

Rich though it was in poets and prose authors, Dravidian literature was not productive of historians in the modern acceptance of the term. Such legends as have been handed down from remote antiquity record marvellous happenings, that were probably based upon fact, but in which the supernatural predominates to a confusing extent. The result is that they appeal more to the faith than to the logic of the student. The history of South India only begins with the Hindu dynasties. It opens at an epoch when Aryan ideas and conceptions had commenced to make their influence felt. Three great kingdoms are mentioned, those of the Pandyans, Cholas and Cheras believed to have been founded by three brothers. Of these the Cholas derived their distinguishing title from Shozham, southern. Their domain was designated Chola mandalam, which, under its corrupted form of Coromandel, is still applied by foreigners to that portion of the coast washed by the Bay of Bengal. These three dominant powers were constantly at war. They were perpetually fighting among themselves, and with the innumerable petty kingdoms whereby they were surrounded.

Some time prior to the Christian era Tondaimandalam was absorbed by the expanding power of the Pallavas, a sovereign people whose capital was at Conjeeveram, 40 miles south-west of Madras. They were defeated by the Chalukyans about the 5th century A. D. A subsequent marriage between a Chalukyan princess and a Chola king brought Tondaimandalam into the latter kingdom in the 11th century, at which era the South of India enjoyed such wealth that gold is stated to have been the most common of the precious metals.

CHRISTIANS.

If credence may be placed in the tradition that St. Thomas, the "Doubting Apostle," lived and died at Mylapore on the Coromandel Coast, Christianity was established in Tondaimandalam during the first century of our era. A Greek merchant, who visited the southern part of the Peninsula early in the 6th century A. D., mentioned the large number of Nestorian, or Syrian Christians whom he had found there. He described them as subject to the Bishop of Sileucia, and attributed their conversion to missionaries from Persia.

MUHAMMADANS.

It is claimed that the Raja of Kerala was converted to the Moslem faith in the 9th century, whence dates the Muhammadan population of the West Coast known as Moplahs. In 1294 a Muhammadan army, led by Alla-ud-Din, nephew of the Delhi Emperor, invaded the Deccan and laid siege to Berar and Devagiri. The Raja of the latter place was made prisoner and compelled to pay a heavy ransom. Subsequently the conquerors renamed the city Daulatabad. The Mussulmans penetrated as far south as Tanjore and Madura in their various raids, plundering and laying waste the country. Anarchy followed their retirement. Before long the various Governors appointed by the invaders rebelled against the Delhi Emperor, thus founding the different Muhammadan kingdoms of the Deccan. The first to succeed was the Viceroy of Daulatabad, with whom originated the Bahminy dynasty of Gulburga, in 1347. The Imand Shahi dynasty of Berar was proclaimed in 1484, and the Adil Shahi dynasty of Bijapur in 1489. The Nizam Shahi dynasty of Ahmadnagar was established at about the same period: The Bareed Shahi dynasty of Bidar dates from 1498, and the Kutab Shahi dynasty of Golcondah from 1512. The present Muhammadan State of Hyderabad is of comparatively recent growth, having been founded as late as the 18th century by Azaf Jah, a minister of the Delhi Emperor Ferukhsir, who, in 1713, appointed him Governor of the Deccan, with the title of Nizam-ul-Mulk. Under the Emperor Muhammad Shah, Azaf Jah was recalled, and promoted Grand Wazir, a post which he resigned. Returning to the Deccan in 1723 he proceeded to take advantage of the weak condition of the central power to found the independent principality still ruled over by the Nizams of Hyderabad.

VIJIANAGAR.

While the various Muhammadan Governors were busily engaged in establishing themselves as monarchs in the Deccan, the shattered Hindu powers rallied sufficiently to organise a formidable empire south of the Kistna. This was ruled over by the Vijianagar dynasty founded in 1336 by two brothers, Harihara and Bukka, the sons of a Carnatic Chief, said to have been of Korumber descent. They built their capital on the south bank of the Tungabhadra River. It included Hampi, already sacred and classical ground, as forming part of Kishindhyah. The site selected was a plain, admirably defended by hills, with openings to east and west. Bukka was the first sovereign of the line. His reign extended from 1336 until 1367, when he was succeeded by his son. It was soon the paramount power in Southern India. Contemporary writers have left glowing accounts of its wealth and opulence. That these were not mere traveller's tales, coloured according to fancy, is testified by the vast and magnificent sculptured remains which still exist of the erstwhile capital. Finally, in 1564, the Muhammadan Sultans of the Deccan combined to overthrow the great Hindu dynasty. The battle of Tellakottah proved fatal. Ram Raja was slain. His fabulously rich city was plundered and reduced to ruins, and his family forced to fly for their lives. Two of his brothers escaped. One established himself at Penoocondah, and the other at Chandragiri, 70 miles north-west of Madras. At the latter place the last king boasting any power caused a gold plated kaul to be executed conveying the site of Fort St. George to Francis Day, as Agent of the East India Company. This was the final act of his reign. Shortly afterwards he was mulcted of his remaining sovereignty by the Sultan of Golcondah. His descendants were reduced to an obscure existence at Anagundi.

It was a curious fiat of destiny which ordained that the last royal act of the last Vijianagar sovereign should be to lay the foundation stone of the British-Indian Empire.

GOVERNORS OF FORT ST. GEORGE.

AGENTS.

Andrew Cogan	...	...	...	1640	
Francis Day	...	...	...	1643	
Thomas Ivie	...	...	...	1644	
Henry Greenhill	...	...	...	1648	

PRESIDENT.

Aaron Baker	...	...	...	1652	

AGENTS.

Henry Greenhill	...	...	...	1655	
Sir Thomas Chamber	...	...	...	1659	
Sir Edward Winter	...	...	...	1661	
Mr. George Foxcroft	...	...	...	1665	

GOVERNORS.

Mr. George Foxcroft appointed first Governor, Fort St. George	...	...	...	1666	
Sir William Langhorn, Bart.		...	...	1670	
Mr. Streynsham Master	...	...	...	1678	
Mr. William Gyfford	...	...	...	1681	
Mr. Elihu Yale	...	...	...	1684	*Acting.*
Mr. William Gyfford	...	...	...	1685	
Mr. Elihu Yale	...	...	...	1687	
Mr. Nathaniel Higginson		...	...	1692	
Mr. Thomas Pitt	...	...	...	1698	
Mr. Gulstone Addison	...	...	...	1709	
Mr. Edmond Montague	...	...	...	1709	*Acting.*
Mr. William Fraser	...	...	...	1709	*Acting.*
Mr. Edward Harrison	...	...	...	1711	
Mr. Joseph Collet	...	...	...	1717	
Mr. Francis Hastings	...	...	...	1720	*Acting.*

Mr. Nathaniel Elwick	...	...	...	1721
Mr. James Macrae	...	...	...	1725
Mr. George Morton Pitt	...	...	...	1730
Mr. Richard Benyon	...	...	...	1735
Mr. Nicholas Morse	...	...	...	1744
Mr. John Hinde	...	...	...	–
Mr. Charles Floyer	...	...	...	1747
Mr. Thomas Saunders	...	...	...	1750
Mr. George Pigot	...	...	...	1755
Mr. Robert Palk	...	...	...	1763
Mr. Charles Bourchier	...	...	...	1767
Mr. Josias Du Pre	...	...	...	1770
Mr. Alexandar Wynch	...	...	...	1773
Lord Pigot ...	...	...	...	1775 *Second Appointment.*
Mr. George Stratton	...	...	...	1776
Mr. John Whitehill	...	...	...	1777 *Acting.*
Mr. Thomas Rumbold	...	...	...	1778
Mr. John Whitehill	...	...	...	1780 *Acting.*
Mr. Charles Smith	..	...	...	1780 *Acting.*
Lord Macartney	...	...	...	1781
Mr. Alexander Davidson	...	...	...	1785 *Acting.*
Major-General Sir Archibald Campbell, K. B.			...	1786
Mr. John Holland	...	...	...	1789
Mr. Edward Holland	...	...	...	1790 *Acting.*
Major-General William Medows		...	...	1790
Sir Charles Oakley, Bart		...	...	1792
Lord Hobart	...	...	...	1794
Lieut.-General George Harris		...	...	1798 *Acting.*
Lord Clive ...	...	...	...	1798
Lord William Cavendish Bentinck		...	...	1803
Mr. William Petrie	...	...	...	1807 *Acting.*
Sir George Hilaro Barlow, Bart., K.C.B.			...	1807
Lieut.-General the Hon'ble John Abercromby			...	1813
Mr. Hugh Elliot	...	...	...	1814
Major-General Sir Thomas Munro, Bart., K.C.B.				1820
Mr. Henry Sullivan Graeme		...	...	1827
Mr. Stephen Rumbold Lushington		...	...	1827
Lieut.-General Sir Frederick Adam, K. C. B.			...	1832
Mr. George Edward Russell		...	...	1837 *Acting*
Lord Elphinstone	...	...	..	1837

The Marquis of Tweedale, *Kt.*	1842	
Mr. Henry Dickinson	1848	*Acting.*
Major-General Sir Henry Pottinger	1848	
Mr. Daniel Eliott	1854	*Acting.*
Lord Harris	1854	
Sir Charles Edward Trevelyan, K.C.B. ...	1859	
Mr. William Ambrose Morehead	1860	*Acting.*
Sir Henry George Ward, *Kt.*	1860	
Mr. William Ambrose Morehead	1860	*Acting. Second Time*
Colonel Sir William Thomas Denison, K.C.B. ...	1861	
Mr. Edward Maltby	1863	
Lord Napier of Mershistoun	1866	
Mr. Alexander John Arbuthnot, C.S.I. ...	1872	*Acting.*
Lord Hobart	1872	
Mr. William Rose Robinson, C.S.I.	1875	*Acting.*
The Duke of Buckingham and Chandos, G.C.S.I.	1875	
Mr. William Patrick Adam	1880	
Mr. William Huddleston, C.S.I.	1881	*Acting.*
Mr. Mountstuart Elphinstone Grant Duff ...	1881	
The Hon'ble Robert Bourke, G.C.I.E. ...	1886	
Mr. John Henry Garstin, C.S.I.	1890	*Acting.*
Lord Wenlock, G.C.I.E.	1891	
Sir Arthur Elibank Havelock, G.C.M.G., G.C.I.E.	1896	
Mr. Arthur Oliver Villiers, Baron Ampthill, G.C.I.E.	1900	
Sir James Thomson, M.A., K.C.S.I., I.C.S. ...	1904	*Acting.*
Mr. Arthur Oliver Villiers, Baron Ampthill, G.C.S.I., G.C.I.E.	1904	
Sir Arthur Lawley, G.C.I.E., K.C.M.G. ...	1906	
Sir Thomas David Gibson-Carmichael, Bart., G.C.I.E., G.C.M.G.	1911	
Sir Murray Hammick, K.C.S.I., C.I.E., I.C.S ...	1912	*Acting.*
Lord Pentland, P.C., G.C.I.E.	1912	
Sir Alexandar Cardew	1919	*Acting.*
Lord Willingdon	1919	

RATES FOR CONVEYANCES

A variety of conveyances are used in Madras. Those classed hackney carriages come under the heading of jutkas, Bandies, Rickshaws as well as a species of four-wheeled Victoria.

The rates are as follows:—

Time	Pair horse carriage	Carriage drawn by a single horse or pair of ponies		Jutka and pair bullock carriages	Single bullock carriages and rickshaws
		1st class	2nd class		
	Rs. A. P.	Rs. A. P.	Rs. A. P.	Rs. A. P.	Rs. A. P.
Per day (6 a.m. to 6 p.m. ...	7 0 0	4 0 0	3 0 0	2 0 0	1 8 0
Per half-day (6 a.m. to 12 noon, 12 noon to 6 p.m. 6 p.m. to 12 p.m.) ...	4 0 0	2 0 0	1 8 0	1 0 0	0 12 0
Per trip: 1st mile ...	1 0 0	0 12 0	0 8 0	0 4 0	0 2 0
Per trip: For every subsequent mile ...	0 8 0	0 6 0	0 4 0	0 2 0	0 1 0
Rate of speed ...	6 miles an hour	5 miles an hour	5 miles an hour	4 miles an hour	3 miles an hour
Every fifteen minutes detention ...	0 4 0	0 2 0	0 2 0	0 1 0	0 1 0

No tariff exists for motor cars which ply for hire. Travellers should arrange beforehand with the driver.